CULTURE SMART!
MOROCCO

Jillian York

·K·U·P·E·R·A·R·D·

ISBN 978 1 85733 337 4
This book is also available as an e-book: eISBN 978 1 85733 571 2

British Library Cataloguing in Publication Data
A CIP catalogue entry for this book is available from the British Library

Copyright © 2006 Kuperard
Revised 2009; fourth printing 2011

First published in Great Britain 2006
by Kuperard, an imprint of Bravo Ltd
59 Hutton Grove, London N12 8DS
Tel: +44 (0) 20 8446 2440   Fax: +44 (0) 20 8446 2441
www.culturesmart.co.uk
Inquiries: sales@kuperard.co.uk

Distributed in the United States and Canada
by Random House Distribution Services
1745 Broadway, New York, NY 10019
Tel: +1 (212) 572-2844   Fax: +1 (212) 572-4961
Inquiries: csorders@randomhouse.com

Series Editor Geoffrey Chesler
Design Bobby Birchall

Printed in Malaysia

Cover image: Traditional woven carpet, Marrakech.
Travel Ink/Chris Stammers
The imges on pages 16, 17, 36, 93, 72, and 114 are reproduced by permission of the author.

About the Author

JILLIAN YORK is an American teacher and writer who lives and works in Morocco. A graduate of Binghamton University with a B.A. in Sociology, specializing in North African and Middle Eastern Studies, she studied Arabic at Al Akhawayn University in Ifrane, Morocco, as part of her degree course. She currently teaches English as a foreign language at the American Language Center of Meknès.

The Culture Smart! series is continuing to expand.
For further information and latest titles visit
www.culturesmartguides.com

The publishers would like to thank **CultureSmart!**Consulting for its help in researching and developing the concept for this series.

CultureSmart!Consulting creates tailor-made seminars and consultancy programs to meet a wide range of corporate, public-sector, and individual needs. Whether delivering courses on multicultural team building in the USA, preparing Chinese engineers for a posting in Europe, training call-center staff in India, or raising the awareness of police forces to the needs of diverse ethnic communities, it provides essential, practical, and powerful skills worldwide to an increasingly international workforce.

For details, visit www.culturesmartconsulting.com

CultureSmart!Consulting and **CultureSmart!** guides have both contributed to and featured regularly in the weekly travel program "Fast Track" on BBC World TV.

contents

contents

Map of Morocco

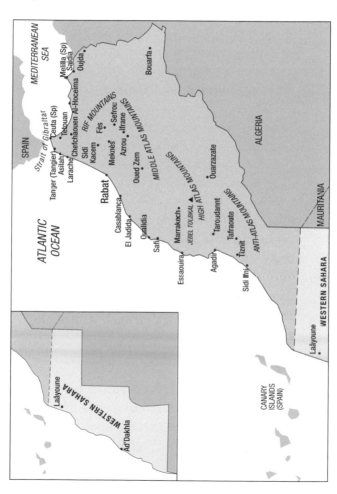

introduction

Morocco is a land of vivid contrasts. The gateway to two continents, it is a country of spectacular landscapes, rich in history, and heady with sumptuous scents and breathtaking sights. While the countryside is home to ancient traditions and diverse peoples, the ever-growing urban centers boast incredible new architecture alongside the old, and activities to suit all modern tastes.

In the crowded ancient *medinas*, young men in designer jeans haggle over cell phones alongside traditionally dressed women shopping for housewares. In the fertile countryside, a farmer riding on a goat is as common a sight as a television satellite perched on a mud-brick roof. Moroccan culture is difficult to pigeonhole. It is a unique blend of Arab, African, and European ways of life, and the Moroccans wouldn't have it any other way.

After 1956, when Morocco was granted independence from colonial rule by France, the country was jolted into the twentieth century. Religious faith and traditional ways of life were forced to contend with Western ideals and norms introduced by the former colonists, and the Moroccan people had to adjust. Fortunately, Moroccans are incredibly adaptable and have managed to hold on to their values while moving forward.

The Moroccans are warm, hospitable, and open-minded, but for the uninitiated, there can be plenty of snares and snags along the road to acceptance. *Culture Smart! Morocco* aims to start you on the path to understanding this sometimes frustrating, yet rich and fascinating culture. The brief historical overview provides an insight into the way the past has helped shape modern Moroccan values and attitudes. There are chapters on customs and traditions, and on the complexities of modern Moroccan life, with advice on what to expect and how to behave appropriately in different situations. For the business traveler there is practical guidance on how to get things done, and how to make the most of the opportunities that present themselves.

Though Morocco has its share of problems—for example, the dispute over the Western Sahara and a high unemployment rate—Moroccans are as loyal to their king as they are to God, a fact that is epitomized in the country's motto: "*God, the Country, the King.*" They are also fiercely loyal to family, but they will welcome you into their inner circle if, by showing flexibility and respect, you allow them.

Key Facts

Official Name	*Al-Mamlakah al-Maghribiyah* (Kingdom of Morocco)	Morocco is an associate member of the European Union.
Capital City	Rabat (population approx. 1.4 million)	
Main Cities	Casablanca (official population is approx. 3.8 million, but with the surrounding areas could be as high as 5 million)	Smaller cities: Fès, Meknes, Tangier, Marrakech, Oujda.
Population	Approx. 31 million	
Area	267,930 sq. miles (446,550 sq. km)	
Terrain	Mountain ranges, incl. the Atlas Mountains, run NE–SW; fertile coastal plains in W	
Climate	Varies significantly. Four general climates: Desert (hot with little precipitation) Mediterranean (mild winters, temperate summers) Middle Atlas and mountains (hot dry summers, cold winters) High mountain (cold and snowy in winter, hot and dry in summer, with cold nighttime temperatures)	
Language	Arabic, spoken in Maghrebi dialect (*derija*). French is also widely spoken.	Modern Standard Arabic is used in the media and religion, and Spanish is spoken in the north.
Religion	98% of Moroccans are Sunni Muslim.	Other religions: Judaism and Christianity

Government	Constitutional monarchy	Executive power is in the hands of the parliament. A prime minister and ministers are appointed and are answerable to the King and parliament.
Currency	Moroccan dirham (MAD or dh)	It is illegal to export Moroccan dirhams.
Media	2M and TVM are the national TV networks. There are a few local and many satellite stations. National newspapers are available in both French and Arabic.	There is no English-language newspaper, but international papers and magazines in English are available.
Electricity	220V (50Hz). Some older buildings may still use 110V electricity.	Two-prong European plugs are used.
DVD/Video	Morocco uses the SECAM system for TV/video, which is also used by France.	DVD is European-region; however, many DVDs are not legal copies and are therefore playable on all regional players.
Internet Domain	.ma	
Telephone	Morocco's country code is 212.	To dial out of Morocco, use 00 and then the country code.
Time Zone	GMT	Morocco does not observe Daylight Saving Time.

chapter one

LAND & PEOPLE

GEOGRAPHICAL SNAPSHOT

Morocco is one of three countries—along with Algeria and Tunisia—that make up North Africa, or the Maghreb (meaning "the West" in Arabic). Approximately the size of Sweden, it is still primarily a rural country. With a population of some 31 million, Morocco has only two cities with a population of over 1 million and only three more that approach this figure.

Geographically, Morocco is both "the gateway to Africa" for Western travelers and "the gateway to Europe" for many Moroccans. Across the Strait of Gibraltar, it is only some 8 miles (13 km) from Spain; in the east, it borders Algeria; in the south, the disputed Western Sahara and, beyond, Mauritania; and to the west, the Atlantic Ocean. While Morocco has no overseas territories, it contains within its borders two Spanish exclaves, Ceuta (or Sebta, in Arabic) and Melilla.

Morocco boasts over 2,200 miles (3,540 km) of coastline bordering the Mediterranean and the Atlantic Oceans. It is also home to four mountain ranges—the rugged Rif Mountains in the north; the Middle and High Atlas, which create a natural division between the coastal regions and the Sahara; and the Saharan Anti-Atlas range. Morocco boasts North Africa's highest peak, Jebel Toubkal (13,650 feet, or 4,160 meters).

The varied landscape includes sandy desert, stony steppes, over 500,000 acres (202,343 ha.) of cedar forest and, most notably, argan forests. The squat and heavily fruited argan tree is indigenous to Morocco and grows mostly in the south. Argan oil, which is used for cooking and is extremely time-consuming to produce, is exported to several countries at a handsome profit.

CLIMATE

Due to its long coastline and its mountain ranges, Morocco has the most varied climate in all of North Africa. Summers are hot and dry while late fall and spring are rainy. Snow falls consistently in

the Middle Atlas regions surrounding Azrou and Ifrane during winter, and across all of the high mountain peaks. While Marrakech may be comfortably warm in midwinter, one can see

the snowcapped peaks of the High Atlas from the city. Particularly notable are the winds: *chergui,* a dry southeasterly wind, and *gharbi* (from *gharb,* meaning west), a cold wet westerly wind. They are responsible for both rain and drought in Morocco.

TEMPERATURE RANGES		
	High (June–August)	**Low** (December–February)
South	38°C/100°F	5°C/41°F
Middle Atlas	32°C/90°F	5°C/41°F
Coastal	28°C/82°F	8°C/47°F
Mediterranean	28°C/82°F	9°C/48°F

CITIES
Casablanca
Morocco's largest city is Casablanca, with a population of approximately 3.8 million. This cosmopolitan city is now the country's industrial capital, though for its size and scope, it has a surprisingly brief history—most of the buildings

date from the years of the French protectorate. There is a small *medina* (walled Islamic city, as found in most Moroccan cities), which provides evidence of its former existence as a provincial town. The most striking landmark in Casa, as it is commonly known, is the Hassan II Mosque, built in 1999 and paid for almost entirely by public donations (at a price tag of more than half a billion U.S. dollars). Its minaret is 689 feet (210 meters) high and its workings are strikingly high-tech, including centrally heated floors and a retractable roof.

Rabat

Most foreign residents live in Casablanca and Rabat (population approximately 1.4 million), Casablanca's equally modern sister and the current capital of Morocco. Rabat's modern downtown is somewhat reminiscent of Paris—if the French capital were to have palm trees and year-round sun. The city has a fine *medina*, dating back to the seventeenth century.

Rabat is perhaps more refined than Casablanca, and is home to some excellent restaurants, as well as several American and European fast-food chains, and to plenty of nightlife, mostly of the upscale variety. The city is also home to the majority of foreign embassies, though some consulates are located in Casablanca.

Marrakech

One of Morocco's former imperial capitals, Marrakech (pop. 970,000) is no less glorious today. Its ochre buildings (the city authorities have stipulated that all new buildings must also be this color—even McDonald's fits the

mold!) and medieval sights make it a unique tourist destination, but the city is also quite modern and chic in its own right. Every fall, it is home to a film festival that attracts both Moroccan and Hollywood filmmakers and stars.

Fès

Fès (also spelled Fez; pop. 1 million) is the oldest of the former imperial capitals and has long been considered the center of both Islam and cultural sophistication in Morocco. Its ancient *medina* is unique in that it is one of the largest living medieval cities in the world. Here, one can stroll through the streets and encounter ancient customs and entirely modern workings side by side—it is not uncommon to see an old man followed by a donkey, with the donkey straining under a case of

Coca-Cola. The Fez Medina Project (www.fesmedina.com) is working to restore the area, which is struggling under the burden of its million or more citizens. UNESCO has declared Fès a World Heritage Site, and is also working to preserve the ancient city.

Meknès

Only an hour west of Fès, Meknès is another former imperial capital; however, the cities are as different as night and day. While Fès teems with life and spirituality, Meknès is slower and calmer, and its inhabitants are friendly and welcoming. There are few foreign residents here, though the total population of the greater Meknès area is thought to be around 1 million. Meknès is split between its *medina* and imperial city and the new, French-built *ville nouvelle* (new town), which contains modern creature comforts such as a brand new supermarket. Meknès is situated near two of Morocco's most important historic sites—

the Roman ruins of Volubilis and the holy town of Moulay Idriss. It is surrounded by vast areas of agricultural land, rich in olives (and olive oil), grains, and grapes for wine. Aicha, a large company that produces oils, jellies, and

other cooking supplies, is based outside Meknès
as is the Les Celliers de Meknès winery.

Ifrane

Ifrane, by no means a large city, is only of interest to
foreigners because of its prestigious English-
language university, Al Akhawayn (www.aui.ma).
The university, founded in 1995 by King Hassan II
and King Fahd of Saudi Arabia, caters mainly to the
children of wealthy Moroccans; classes are in
English and are based on the American system.
Various areas of study are offered at undergraduate
and graduate levels, and the university hosts many
foreign employees and exchange students. In the
summer there is an intensive Arabic program,
which is of interest to anyone planning to remain in
Morocco for some time.

A BRIEF HISTORY

Though Morocco has only been an independent
state since 1956, its history is as rich and complex
as its people. Over time and due to its prime
location, the influences of various cultures have
shaped Morocco, ultimately contributing to its
fabulous diversity. The following is only a brief
snapshot of the country's fascinating past, but it
provides a glimpse into the ancient culture that
gave birth to present-day Morocco.

The Original Moroccans

Indigenous to Morocco are the people now known as the Berbers, also referred to as *Imazighen* (sing. *Amazigh*). Little is known of their origins, though they probably came from southwest or central Asia as early as 10,000 BCE. They are thought to have migrated over time to North Africa, where they inhabited the Mediterranean coastline from Egypt to the Atlantic. Berbers today vary greatly in physical appearance as a result of thousands of years of mixing with other ethnic groups.

"Berber" is the ancient Arabic name for the inhabitants of North Africa, perhaps from the word *barbara*, meaning "those who babble confusedly" (which may itself be derived from the Greek *barbaria*). The Berbers were, and to a degree remain, a tribal people. They have clung to their tribal identity, as well as to a traditional pastoral mountain existence or a nomadic desert one. Centered around clan and tribe, ancient Berber society was relatively isolated until the rise of the great Mediterranean empires.

Phoenicians, Greeks, and Romans

In the first millennium BCE, Phoenician traders spread across the North African coast, establishing their capital at Carthage (present-day Tunis). They founded the settlements of Tingis (Tangier), Mogador (Essaouira), Tamuda (Tetouan), and

Lixus (Larache). They were followed shortly afterward by the Greeks, who settled in various locations across North Africa. It wasn't until the Punic Wars, fought against Rome in the third century BCE, that the Carthaginians were finally defeated.

Though Carthage was successfully defended in the First Punic War (264–241 BCE), the Second Punic War (218–201 BCE) found the Romans controlling local leaders and constructing new settlements. In the Third Punic War (149–146 BCE) Carthage was destroyed and its possessions became the Roman province of Africa. The city of Volubilis, just outside modern Meknès, became an important outpost of the Roman Empire. It is the best-preserved Roman ruin in Morocco, and was declared a UNESCO World Heritage Site in 1997.

Throughout these conquests, many Berbers, who were concentrated in mountain areas where others dared not venture, continued to live in the manner to which they had been accustomed for centuries. Those traders who came into contact with them formed mutually beneficial alliances.

With the fall of Rome at the end of the fifth century, the Byzantines and the Vandals both attempted to fill the power vacuum, but to no avail; Berber tribes succeeded in recovering their land, at least for some time.

Arab Conquest and Islamization

With the death of the Prophet Mohammed in 632 CE, Islam began its westward spread and by the end of the century conquering Arab armies had arrived in Morocco. Many Berbers welcomed the security provided by these latest invaders and converted to Islam, molding it to their own cultural traditions.

Rather than move on as their predecessors had done, the Arabs stayed in Morocco, expanding trade ties and opening overland caravan routes across the Sahara. They allowed Berbers into the ranks of the military and into politics, provided they were willing to embrace Islam; for the Berbers, therefore, the incentive to convert was not only spiritual.

In theory, the Maghreb was under the rule of the Caliphate in Baghdad. However, Berbers and Arabs alike chose to adapt Islam to local conditions, and established an independence that was to continue for centuries. Morocco would never again come under the rule of the East— not even that of the Ottoman Empire.

Moroccan Dynasties

The great Arab historian and philosopher Ibn Khaldun (1332–1402) based his model of dynastic cycles on this next period of Moroccan history. He saw a constant conflict between the cities and the countryside and demonstrated that the Berber kingdoms had a tendency to rise and fall over a similar pattern. The rural Berbers were drawn periodically to the easier life of settled areas, and thus to the conquest of towns. The vigorous first generation of rulers continued to live an austere and simple lifestyle, the second adapted to urban culture, and the third generation, removed from its roots, succumbed to internal conflict. The fourth and final generation saw their subjects as sources of wealth that could be drained to expand the empire, but ultimately this process was too rapid to be sustained. Their collapse left a power vacuum that another rural-based dynasty would then fill.

The Idrissids (789–985)

The founder of the first Moroccan dynasty was Idriss I, a Shiite political exile from Mecca who established himself outside the ancient Roman city of Volubilis in the eighth century. The northern Awraba tribe of Berbers found an ally in Moulay Idriss and recruited him as their *imam* (religious leader). Soon the Idrissid dynasty was dominant throughout northern Morocco. After the assassination of Idriss I by his sworn enemies, his son succeeded him as *imam* at the age of eleven. Idriss II built an impressive capital, Fès, thus creating the first Moroccan state. The Idrissids were overthrown by Berbers in the tenth century and Morocco broke up once more into small tribal states.

The Almoravids (1073–1146)

This state of anarchy came to an end when the Almoravids rose to power in the eleventh century. A *mélange* of three Berber tribes from the Sahara, they founded Marrakech as their capital before moving north to create an empire that embraced Morocco, parts of Algeria, and Spain. The Almoravid dynasty adhered to a fiercely fundamentalist form of Islam; "*Almoravid*" literally means "veiled ones" and comes from the Almoravids' practice of wearing a veil across the face.

The Almohads (1147–1269)

True to Ibn Khaldun's model, the Almoravids soon fell and were succeeded by a rival Berber dynasty, the sectarian Shiite Almohads. The new dynasty kept Marrakech as the capital. They built the famed Koutoubia Mosque and extended the empire eastward, but their piety soon waned— corruption once again took hold, the dynasty weakened, and later they lost most of Spain.

The Merenids (1269–1465)

The successors to the Almohads were the Merenids, a group of nomadic Zanata Berbers, who seized Marrakech in 1269. The Merenids never managed to achieve the opulence of their predecessors but did manage to last for two centuries, ruling all of Morocco.

The Saadians (1554–1629)

In the sixteenth century the Moroccan empire split into two separate kingdoms, based in Fès and Marrakech. In 1492 the last Muslims were expelled from the Iberian Peninsula, and in the fifteenth century Spain and Portugal captured and occupied Morocco's ports. Resistance to the Christian threat was led by religious leaders, one of whom established the Saadian dynasty in 1554. The Saadians were Sharifians, tribal descendants of the Prophet. Ahmed al-Mansour ("the Victorious") restored the unity of Morocco and defeated Sebastian, King of Portugal, decisively at the Battle of the Three Kings, where he was proclaimed Sultan in 1578. He repelled a Turkish invasion, conquered the Sudan, and named Marrakech his capital, adorning it with marble.

The Alawites (1666–)

The death of Sultan al-Mansour in 1603 led to a long struggle for the succession. The Alawites

were the next to step up to the throne. They too
were Sharifians, and Moulay Rashid was their first
leader. On his death, his half brother Moulay
Ismail began his long reign (1672–1727), which
signaled a new era for Morocco. Ismail was a cruel
but effective leader. From 1672 he revived
Moroccan power and from his capital of Meknes,
he managed to break the pattern of dynastic
cycles, capturing European-held strongholds and
creating a stable and secure kingdom. Meknes has
often been referred to as the Versailles of
Morocco. The Alawite dynasty still rules today.

The Moors

While Europe was entering the Dark Ages, Arab
civilization was flourishing. In the eighth century,
the combined Berber-Arab armies of Tarik ben
Ziyed crossed the Straits of Gibraltar into Spain. In
Andalucia (Al-Andalus) and elsewhere they created
a sophisticated multiethnic society. Arab scholars
brought with them Arabic translations of the
Greek classics and their own scientific knowledge,
and ushered in a period of cultural and intellectual
cross-fertilization. They established a Caliphate at
Córdoba in 929 that was independent of Baghdad.
In the eleventh century, the Almoravids were called
in from Morocco to help defend the city from
Christian attack and stayed to reform Islam in the
region. The Almohads followed in the twelfth

century, remaining until they were ousted by the
Castilian *conquistadores* at the Battle of Toledo in
1212. The Catholic *reconquista* of Spain continued
for several centuries until the fall of the last
independent Muslim kingdom, Granada, in 1492.

Both Muslims and Sephardic (Spanish) Jews
sought asylum and were welcomed in Morocco,
where their skills and talents were appreciated.
Many resettled in Salé and Rabat.

European Advances

Most of Morocco's ports, we have seen, had been
captured by Spain and Portugal by the beginning
of the fifteenth century. In the nineteenth century
Morocco's sovereignty was further eroded as its
strategic importance and economic potential
attracted the interest of Europe's imperial powers.
In 1854 Sultan Abd ar-Rahman, who supported
the Algerians in their war with France, was
defeated at the Battle of Isly. In 1856, under

British pressure, he opened Morocco to European commerce. In 1860 Spain invaded, and Morocco was forced to cede it the southwestern region of Ifni. In 1880 the major European powers and the United States agreed at the Madrid Conference to preserve the territorial integrity of Morocco and to maintain equal trade opportunities for all.

Imperial ambitions soon ended this arrangement. Spain, and ultimately Germany, cast longing eyes at Morocco. France, which had colonized neighboring Algeria, was intent on securing Morocco for itself. Franco-German rivalry caused a major international crisis that led to the 1906 Algeciras Conference, at which the principles of the Madrid Conference were reaffirmed. In 1911 German objections to French influence in Morocco were overcome by territorial compensations in central Africa. Finally, on March 30, 1912, Sultan Abd al-Hafid was compelled to sign the Treaty of Fès, by which nine-tenths of Morocco became a French protectorate, under the rule of General Lyautey. Rabat was declared the capital and the Sultan the figurehead of the Moroccan state, with true control coming from Paris.

The rest of the country was administered by Spain. The Spanish protectorate included Spanish Morocco on the northern coast with Tetouan as its capital, and a Southern Protectorate of Morocco, administered as part of the Spanish Sahara. The port of Tangier was separated from Spanish Morocco and made a neutral international zone.

The Protectorate
France began to develop its new acquisition and more than one hundred thousand French settlers moved into the territory. Resident-General

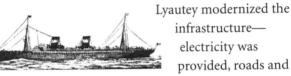

Lyautey modernized the infrastructure— electricity was provided, roads and railways were created, and Casablanca became a major commercial port.

Interestingly, the European colonists never made any real attempt to impose Christianity on Morocco. Although they set up churches for their own use, the French built their own parts of towns, called *villes nouvelles*, keeping out of the *medinas* and leaving the mosques undisturbed.

In 1921 European rule was threatened by a revolt led by Abdelkrim Khattabi, who instigated the Rif War (1921–26) and defeated a large Spanish force at Anoual. The rebels, made up of Rifian Berbers, were eventually crushed by a combined French-Spanish army, led by Marshal Pétain and Francisco Franco, in 1926. In 1934 the Moroccan nationalist movement began political activity.

Independence

French colonial rule lasted for a mere forty-four years. During the Second World War, after the fall of France, Morocco officially remained loyal to the Vichy French government; resistance ended when the Allied forces landed in 1942. The following year, the Allied leaders met at Casablanca. While Charles de Gaulle, head of the Free French Forces at the time, lobbied for the continuation of French rule, the Moroccan Istiqlal (Independence) Party issued a manifesto demanding independence. The Istiqlal Party was comprised of educated urban professionals and students, the products of French modernization and educational reform.

The year 1945 brought famine to Morocco due to the war; while 95 percent of the population lived in the countryside, this "year of hunger" forced them into the cities to find food and work. In 1948 consultative assemblies were introduced. The French outlawed the Istiqlal in 1952, however, and in Fès protestors took to the streets. A bomb that exploded in Casablanca's central market, killing seventeen people and wounding dozens of others, fanned the flames. The French arrested thousands, and in response to Sultan Mohammed V's growing support and encouragement of the party, they deposed and exiled him to Madagascar in 1953.

The French misjudged the consequences of their action. The exile of Sultan Mohammed V was extremely unpopular with the Moroccan populace, and between 1953 and 1955 there were an increasing number of anti-French riots. Random acts of violence against colonists were commonplace. In 1955 a Berber tribe slaughtered the entire French population of the village of Oued Zem, bringing the conflict to its zenith. The summary decision was made to grant Morocco independence. French and Spanish forces withdrew in 1956, and Tangier was given to Morocco by international agreement. Spain ceded the Southern Protectorate in 1958. Mohammed V returned from exile as sovereign in 1956, taking the title of King the following year.

King Hassan II

Hassan II ascended the throne in 1961 after the sudden death of his father and ruled for nearly four decades. At the outset, he

updated his own role, turning Morocco into a constitutional monarchy and creating a parliament. Though opening the door to democracy, he still kept absolute power and several times disbanded parliament and ruled by decree.

Hassan II faced significant opposition during his reign, particularly from Islamists and Nationalists. He survived two assassination attempts, one by General Oufkir, one of his trusted generals. Oufkir's assassination attempt is documented in a book by his daughter Malika, who spent twenty years with the rest of her family in a desert prison for her father's crime.

Despite conflicts at home, Hassan II's involvement in foreign affairs was impressive. In 1969 he secured the return of the Spanish overseas province of Ifni to Morocco. He was a firm advocate of a peaceful solution to the Arab-Israeli conflict. He also showed support for the UN against Saddam Hussein during the first Gulf War. More problematic but nevertheless impressive, in 1975 the king led the famous Green March of more than 350,000 unarmed Moroccan civilians into the Spanish Sahara to reclaim the disputed territory. This move was partly successful—Spain withdrew in 1976, ceding it to Morocco and Mauritania, which quickly bailed out. Morocco moved in to occupy the region, known internationally as the Western Sahara.

CONTEMPORARY MOROCCO

Following the death of Hassan II in 1999, his son, the thirty-five-year-old Mohammed VI, ascended the throne. During his first speech as king, he promised to grant a pardon to 50,000 prisoners. He also fired the infamous head of the security forces known as "the Butcher Basri."

King Mohammed VI has proved to be a progressive monarch. Starting with his 2002 marriage to computer engineer Salma Bennani, he has demonstrated support for women's rights. In 2004 his government made landmark changes to the *Moudawana*, or Family Law, guaranteeing rights for women in the areas of marriage, divorce, and child custody. Incidentally, these laws have sparked another wave of fundamentalism, as there is debate over whether or not aspects of the laws contradict the *Shari'a* (Islamic law).

Morocco is an internationally renowned tourist destination and many foreigners, in search of the exotic, tend to ignore the modern reality of the country. Modern Moroccan culture, however, exists alongside the ancient traditions and is developing rapidly. With 70 percent of the population under the age of thirty, coupled with a 2.2 percent birthrate, Morocco is a young and growing country. Medical technology is allowing for longer lives and has lowered the infant mortality rate significantly in the past decade. The education system is improving and foreign-language education is becoming widespread.

Despite this progress, unemployment hovers at around 20 percent, and more than 50 percent of the population are illiterate. Though the King has promised various reforms, Berbers still suffer significant discrimination—the giving of Berber names to children, forbidden during Hassan II's reign, is still technically illegal and Berber dialects are slowly dying out. On the upside, the King has proposed an Institute for Amazigh (Middle Atlas Berber) Studies, which is slowly coming to fruition, and some schools are beginning to introduce the study of Berber dialects as a subject.

All in all, the reign of King Mohammed VI looks promising. His progressive worldview and Western solidarity have earned him international support, which is crucial at this juncture in Moroccan development.

THE JEWISH LEGACY

Jews are a vital part of Moroccan history. It is widely believed that the first Jews came to the country with the Phoenician traders. Their history is quite complex, but Moroccan Jews lived in relative peace for a long time. Though they were concentrated in *mellahs*, segregated communities not unlike the early ghettos of Europe, they fared comparatively well until the twentieth century.

In 1948 the Jewish population of Morocco numbered around 265,000. Today, fewer than 10,000 remain. Despite hundreds of years of peaceful coexistence, in 1948, in response to events in Palestine, bloody riots broke out in Oujda and Djerada: forty-four Jews were killed and many others were wounded. Jews began to emigrate, the majority to the newly created state of Israel.

In 1956, when Morocco gained independence, Jewish emigration to Israel was suspended. In 1963, following the resumption of emigration, more than 100,000 Moroccan Jews headed east. Over a span of less than fifty years, more than 200,000 Moroccan Jews left their home country.

King Hassan II protected the status of the Jewish population, organizing the first meeting of the World Union of Moroccan Jews in Marrakech in 1999. His support for a peaceful solution to the Arab-Israeli conflict has consolidated Morocco's warm relations with Israel, and Moroccan Jewish émigrés enjoy the freedom to visit Morocco, even if they hold Israeli citizenship.

Though numbering only a few thousand, Jews in Morocco today enjoy relative peace and success. Mostly residing in modern Casablanca, they are indistinguishable from the millions of other residents, except during *Ramadan*, when they can eat in public with impunity. They hold leading positions in government and business.

The major Jewish organization in Morocco is the Conseil des Communautés Israélites (Jewish Community Council), located in Casablanca. It is concerned with external relations as well as community affairs and heritage, and the maintenance of Jewish buildings.

LANGUAGE AND CULTURE

Morocco's linguistic history plays a distinct role in the class system today. As we will see later, although Arabic is the official language, Arabic and French are both considered to be national languages. The Arabic spoken in Morocco is called *derija*, and is a dialect of Modern Standard Arabic, or *al-Arabiya al-fus'ha*. *Derija* is the language of the masses, of daily transactions, and of most homes. French, on the other hand, is the language of commerce, economics, and the bourgeoisie. Modern Standard Arabic is used for education and government, though French is used in the latter when dealing with international issues or publications. French and Arabic are both used for the media. There are families from

Casablanca and Rabat who speak French in the home, though this is rare outside these two cities.

Finally, Berber, an Afro-Asiatic language (like old Egyptian), is confined to the homes of Berber families and rural tribal communities. You will never hear Berber spoken on the streets. Even though the majority of Morocco's population has some Berber heritage (even the King is half-Berber), there is still a stigma attached to the culture and language, and it is only recently that official programs have been implemented to preserve the quickly disappearing language. One, in Azrou, seeks to preserve the Amazigh dialect of Berber, prominent throughout the Middle Atlas.

Because of this linguistic disparity, a form of class distinction has developed whereby French-speakers are admired for their sophistication yet disdained for speaking the language of the

colonizers. Modern Standard Arabic, while highly respected, is not practical as a language for daily life and although it is the official language, it is rarely spoken in its pure form. *Derija* is by far the most useful and practical language for Moroccans, and a foreigner who takes pains to learn it will reap innumerable benefits.

English is slowly coming into its own as a third (or fourth) language for many Moroccans. Most high schools now offer it, and as more students reach university level, they are afforded the opportunity to study it further. Additionally, all major cities have an American Language Center, and Casablanca and Rabat are home to several other schools offering programs in English.

Regardless of which language you speak or learn, you may become frustrated by a habit of many Moroccans—switching back and forth from Arabic to French and even to English. *Derija* is peppered with French-influenced words, and very recently English words have begun to seep in as hip-hop culture and satellite television spread throughout the country.

GOVERNMENT

In 1957, a year after Moroccan independence, Sultan Mohammed V chose the title of King, a title retained by the next two rulers, Hassan II and the present king, Mohammed VI. Morocco is officially a constitutional monarchy. However, the King retains ultimate legal authority and the ability to override aspects of government if necessary. The King is both head of state and religious leader (*amir al-muminin*). He appoints the head of government — the prime minister — and the Council of Ministers.

In 1992 the constitution was amended to increase the influence of parliament. In 1996 a new two-chamber assembly was approved. The 270 members of the upper house, or Chamber of Advisors, are elected indirectly by local councils, professional organizations, and labor syndicates

for a term of nine years. The 325 members of the lower house, the Chamber of Representatives, are elected by popular vote for a term of five years (295 by multiseat constituencies, and 30 from national lists of women). The King can disband parliament by royal decree if necessary.

Morocco's constitution enshrines a multiparty system. The number of parties essentially ensures that no one party will ever gain complete control.

MAJOR POLITICAL PARTIES

Socialist Union of Popular Forces (USFP): social democratic

Istiqlal (Independence): Islamist nationalist

Justice and Development Party (PJD): Islamist

National Rally of Independents (RNI): royalist

Popular Movement (MP): moderate (rural)

The constitution also guarantees all men and women over the age of eighteen the right to vote. Parliament legislates criminal, civil, and commercial law and is essentially in place to approve the King's decrees.

The legal system is based on Islamic law, and on French and Spanish civil law. The highest court in the land is the Supreme Court. Judges are appointed on the recommendation of the Supreme Council of the Judiciary, presided over by the monarch.

Administration

Morocco is divided into sixteen *wilayas*, or regions, including Laayoune and Dakhla in the "Saharan Provinces." These regions are each governed by a *wali*, as well as a governor. The *wali* represents the King; he is responsible for the regional budget, and in an emergency he can summon both the army and the *gendarmerie* (rural police). In addition to the sixteen regions, there are twenty-one prefectures and thirty-three provinces, most of which have a governor.

THE WESTERN SAHARA

The disputed Western Sahara is one of the most sparsely populated regions in the world and consists primarily of desert flatlands. After Spain relinquished control in 1976, Morocco and Mauritania divided the territory between themselves. However, a local independence movement, the Polisario Front, rejected the partition and proceeded to wage guerrilla war from bases in Algeria and later Libya. In 1979 Mauritania withdrew and Morocco annexed its portion of the Western Sahara. Since then Morocco has grappled with Polisario for control of the "Saharan Provinces," and has built a sand and rock wall along the borders to protect it.

In the 1980s Libya and Algeria reduced their support for Polisario, and in 1988 Morocco and Polisario entered into peace talks. In 1991 the two sides agreed to a UN-sponsored cease-fire and to abide by a referendum that would determine once and for all whether the Saharawis actually want independence. The referendum has been postponed numerous times and has yet to be held.

Although today the Western Sahara is recognized as an independent state (the Saharawi Arab Democratic Republic) by forty-four nations and is a member of the African Union, it continues to be administered by Morocco.

RELATIONS WITH THE WEST

Morocco was the first country to recognize the fledgling United States in 1777, and has enjoyed close ties with the U.S.A. ever since. King Mohammed VI supports the global "War on

Terror," which is quite controversial for a Muslim king, especially given the opposition of much of the world. As for European relations, Morocco is an associate member of the European Union, ensuring close ties between the country and its former colonizers. Today Morocco enjoys perhaps the best relations of any Muslim country with the West, particularly since the new king ascended the throne.

chapter two

VALUES & ATTITUDES

Morocco is a country of conflicting values and changing attitudes. Its teeming big cities have an air of sophistication and *joie de vivre*, while the way of life in rural areas has changed little in centuries. And while the cities are suffused with Western culture, tradition and religion still play a vital role in the everyday life of most people.

ISLAM AS A WAY OF LIFE

Morocco is a Muslim country; that is to say all Moroccans—except the fewer than 1 percent who are Jewish—are born Muslim. It is not, however, an Islamic dictatorship, and though the majority of Moroccans practice their religion in one way or another, the country is not entirely run by *Shari'a*, or Islamic law. On the contrary—in recent years, King Mohammed VI has made landmark changes to laws such as the *Moudawana* (Family Law), in a further effort to modernize the country.

On the other hand, one cannot escape the pervasiveness of Islam in Morocco—the more than seven hundred mosques in Fès are proof that this is a pious country. The *adhan*, or call to prayer, beginning with the words "*Allahu Akbar*" or "God is great," sounds from every mosque five times each day—at sunrise, noon, mid-afternoon, sunrise, and evening. On Fridays, the Muslim holy day, many men attend the mosque at noon (even those who do not during the week), and it is not uncommon to see the faithful overflowing onto the streets outside the mosques. Such sidewalks, of course, should be avoided at this time.

Islam, which means "submission" in Arabic, is not simply a religion—it is a way of life. No subject is left out of the Qur'an (Koran), the holy book of Islam. The Qur'an, which was revealed to the Prophet Mohammed at Mecca and Medina in modern-day Saudi Arabia over a period of sixteen years, is considered to be one of the most beautiful works of Arabic literature. In addition to the Qur'an, there are the *hadiths*, or written records of the Prophet's life and sayings, which most Muslims follow in addition to the Qur'an.

The mosque is used for prayer, religious teaching, and community gatherings. Morocco's mosques differ from those in the Middle East and Turkey. Whereas most Middle Eastern mosques are elaborate and domed, with several pointed towers, or minarets, Moroccan mosques generally have one four-sided minaret. Exceptions include the Tin Mal Mosque in Tin Mal (currently under renovation) and the octagonal Grand Mosque in Chefchaouen.

It is important to distinguish between the growth of moderate fundamentalism and the acts of extremism that capture the headlines. In response to the rapid changes taking place in Moroccan society, there has been a move toward conservative values and the strict observance of Islamic practice. Moroccan fundamentalists, however, are often as welcoming of outsiders as their more secular compatriots.

The foreigner in Morocco will often find Islam slowly seeping into his or her life; it is omnipresent in conversation, from the common modifier *insha'Allah* (God willing) used in reference to anything occurring in the future to seemingly random references to Allah. Though at first *insha'Allah* annoys most foreigners—who assume, often correctly, that it is being used to weasel one's way out of a commitment—they usually end up using it themselves. In fact the belief that all events are predestined is quite strong in Islam, and more often than not *insha'Allah* is said in complete earnest. *Maktoub* in Arabic means "it is written" and Moroccans believe that one cannot escape one's destiny. This fatalism manifests itself in different ways, the most visible of which is the seeming reluctance of many Moroccans to improve their lot in life.

Islam will not affect the foreigner's life unless he or she wants it to. Muslims generally don't proselytize; however, if you show an interest in Islam, it is not uncommon for them to try to persuade you to convert. Foreigners are also outside the rules and social structure created by Islam; for example, though Moroccans can be jailed for eating in public during *Ramadan* (though many do eat at home, in private), foreigners are exempt, though they should be discreet. And while Moroccans would never dream of drinking alcohol in public during this month, foreigners are allowed a discreet glass of wine with dinner when it is available.

ISLAMIC EXTREMISM

On May 16, 2003, Morocco's reputation for tolerance was put to the test. Suicide bombers with ties to a radical Islamic group called Salafia Jihadia targeted several sites frequented by foreigners as well as Moroccan Jews. Though this was an isolated incident, it brought to light the radicalizing effects of poverty on sections of the community: the Salafia Jihadia bombers were all youths between the ages of twenty and twenty-four, and several were from an impoverished suburb of Casablanca where fundamentalists had previously tried to impose Islamic law. The police responded vigorously, arresting a number of young men. Salafia Jihadia, however, had international links and was in the news again in 2004 in connection with the Madrid train bombs.

Although the perpetrators believed they were carrying out acts of *jihad* (which literally means "struggle" and can apply to other situations in life as well), the majority of Moroccans were quick to condemn violence in the name of Islam.

Morocco is one of the most liberal Muslim societies, but it is always prudent to be respectful of Islam. Foreigners have complete religious freedom, provided they don't impose their own religion on Muslims. Christians and Jews report few problems, and although Eastern religions are less well known, faith is generally respected. If you have strong views about Islam, it is probably best to keep them to yourself and to prepare stock answers to questions about your own beliefs.

EDUCATION

Education is highly valued in Morocco; however, in a country where unemployment is rife, it is often not the first priority. Children in cities attend either a state-run Moroccan public school or a private school, both of which are based on the French educational model. Classes in public schools are taught in Arabic, with French introduced at the age of eight. Private schools are generally French-language, though  schools using Arabic as the medium of instruction are starting to appear. Secondary school leads to the French baccalaureate, which more students are obtaining each year. The final step is university.

Despite the ideal of "education for all," this is not always achieved. In the countryside, and even sometimes in cities, children—particularly girls—must leave school to help the family.

For foreign residents in Morocco with school-age children, the best bet is to enroll them in a French private school. The only English-language schools are the American Schools in Rabat, Casablanca, and Tangier, and the new George Washington School in Casablanca.

There are seven public universities and one private university in Morocco, and plenty of smaller vocational-type colleges and business schools. The private university, Al Akhawayn ("the two brothers"), was built in 1995 and was funded in part by King Fahd of Saudi Arabia. Classes are conducted entirely in English, and every summer the university plays host to scores of American and European students who come to study Arabic. But the school only caters to the elite, as is apparent from the parking lot full of BMWs and new Volkswagens. The majority of Moroccan students are lucky if they are able to attend university (for although the universities are free of charge, they are all located in major cities and have little accommodation for out-of-town students). Many Moroccans study at foreign universities but again, this  option is limited to the elite and the resourceful. Nevertheless, there has been an upsurge in recent years of Moroccans studying in universities abroad as access to other languages, particularly English, increases.

TORN BETWEEN CULTURES

Situated as it is between Africa and Europe, Morocco has the unfortunate privilege of being caught between cultures as well. On the one hand, there is access to many things Western and new while, on the other, it is rooted in tradition.

There is a broad spectrum of ideals among Moroccans, from the devout Muslim who shuns everything Western to the urban trendsetter wearing designer labels—the majority fall somewhere in the middle. Moroccans are quite fashion-conscious, and even schoolchildren carry cell phones; this is a society that has hit the media age at full throttle, at least in the urban areas. Yet for every cell-phone-wielding ten-year-old you will come across a man who rides a donkey rather than drives a car and for every Moroccan wearing (faux) Dior, you will also see a woman wearing the full veil, revealing only her eyes.

And the country is changing quickly. Just a few years ago, Casablanca and Rabat were the only cities where one could see women dressed in fashionable European styles, smoking in cafés, or wearing bikinis at the pool—now it is not an uncommon sight in smaller cities like Meknes or Tangier. Things are changing, but old habits die hard and traditional values are strong. A surprising first sight for many foreign visitors is the *medina*, where the latest in cell-phone technology is sold alongside traditional handicrafts, and donkeys pass in the narrow streets carrying cases of Coca-Cola.

Young Moroccans are often quick to criticize their elders and each other for having an "odd mentality," but in fact, for a country that has seen so much change in fifty years, it is surprising how quickly most people have adapted. In cyber cafés, old men chat on the Internet alongside young girls, mothers tap their feet to their sons' hip-hop music, and parents tolerate their children's designer jeans and trendy Western hairstyles. While many older women still wear the traditional *djellaba* and *hijab* (more on this below and in Chapter 5), even *hijab*-clad young girls keep up with the latest fashions, albeit opting for the more conservative styles. The older generation has adapted incredibly well to the influx of technology, and in cities, many of the elders tote cell phones.

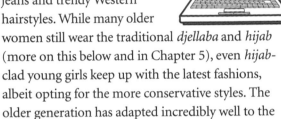

It is often surprising to hear Moroccans' perceptions of foreign countries, particularly the United States—the uninformed listener would be led to believe that in America money grows on trees and everyone is able to afford travel, expensive clothes, and technology.

What does all of this mean? For many young Moroccans, the modernization of their country means that they will be granted the same opportunities as Western youth—better education, access to technology, and the same modern conveniences, to name but a few. Unfortunately for Morocco, it also means that many young people are choosing to pursue education abroad or emigrate, resulting in a "brain drain." But who could blame them when faced with a 20 percent unemployment rate? On the other hand, foreign investment is increasing, and government policies are geared to keep up with the changing times.

PUBLIC VS. PRIVATE SPHERE

There is a huge contrast between public and private behavior. On the street, the rule is everyone for themselves—being there invites attention, and in Moroccan society staring at or approaching a stranger is not considered rude. If you're a woman on the street, you're fair game.

Moroccan women understand the rules of this game and, in order to avoid attention, cover up well out of doors. Even women who do not wear the *hijab* often cover their head loosely with a scarf so as not to attract men on the street. These same women may be wearing designer clothes under their *djellaba* for when they're in the company of women, or their husbands or family. Foreign women who experience harassment in Morocco often do so because of the way they're dressed. This is a source of frustration for Western women, but they will find it easier to conform— in public, that is.

In a culture with such an emphasis on family, it is no surprise that there isn't much value placed on the civil treatment of strangers. Strangers are not people one owes anything to, and so it is not considered necessary to be polite to, say, shopkeepers or café waiters. Still, people in those occupations are very appreciative of the politeness of strangers, though it is not expected.

FAMILY FIRST

The family is perhaps the most important aspect of Moroccan society, and for foreigners, it often takes a bit of getting used to. Family, to a Moroccan, takes precedence over work, friendships, relationships, and sometimes even marriage. For Muslims, it is a duty to obey one's parents, and many Moroccans take this quite seriously. For example, in order to marry, the bridegroom must first ask his parents' permission (regardless of his age). Assuming they consent, he—with parents in tow—must visit his bride-to-be at home and ask the permission of her parents. And although most men don't consider themselves fit to marry until they have a well-paid job and own an apartment or a house, it is not uncommon for newlyweds to live with relatives.

Families generally eat together on a daily basis (made possible by a generous two-hour midday break for most workers and all schoolchildren), and even those living apart from their families try to join them for the Friday meal. Moroccans living far from their family may visit every weekend, or as often as possible, and when taking a vacation, most Moroccans opt to visit extended family rather than stay in an anonymous hotel. If a young person goes off to study at a university in another city, he or she will usually live with members of the extended family, if possible.

HSHUMA

The concept of *hshuma*, or shame, in Moroccan society is important (see also Chapter 8). Family honor is vital and is jealously protected. Unlike Western-style guilt, or the knowledge that *you* have done wrong, *hshuma* is best explained as the knowledge that *others* know that you have done wrong. Therefore, Moroccans will do their best to avoid *hshuma*. This is evident in public behavior. "White lies" (*kdiba bida* in Arabic) are very common—if you were to ask a Moroccan for a favor he could not grant you, for instance, instead of saying no he might postpone the favor indefinitely in order to save face and avoid *hshuma*. No malice is intended.

There are myriad ways in which one can attract *hshuma*. Generally, they all fall into the category of behavior outside the social norms: sexual deviancy, anything forbidden by Islam, and anything forbidden by or unacceptable to one's family bring shame. The shamed person faces ostracism by society or, in serious instances, even by his or her family.

It is worth noting that Moroccans will often go to great lengths for a relative to protect the reputation of the family. Sometimes this is borne out of love, at other times a fear of *hshuma*, but either way, family loyalty is strong; even if one member continuously misbehaves, the family will stand by them as far as possible.

In addition, the way one treats one's friends in public differs greatly from the treatment they receive in private. Praising or thanking your Moroccan friends in public is greatly appreciated, though profuse thanks may be modestly brushed aside. If you find it necessary to reprimand a friend or colleague, it is best done in private, where there is no one to witness the scolding.

It is important to be aware of *hshuma* and to take care not to insult or embarrass your Moroccan friends in public. On the other hand, threatening a Moroccan man with *hshuma* can be an effective way for a woman to get him to leave her alone. "Go to your mother" is one of the worst possible insults, as it reminds him of the *hshuma* his mother would feel if she knew about his behavior.

ATTITUDES TOWARD FOREIGNERS

There is not one particular attitude toward foreigners; rather, it is fair to say that Moroccans are generally both extremely welcoming and extremely curious. *Marhaba* means "welcome" in Arabic, and is a word you will hear repeatedly. Most Moroccans, on learning of a new foreign resident, are incredibly hospitable and will offer their help or invite you to their home for a meal. This hospitality sometimes even extends to tourists, and is, in general, quite genuine. It can be overwhelming for the foreigner, but also quite rewarding.

Unfortunately, there is a downside—in a country with high levels of poverty, where the West is seen as wasteful and extravagant, foreign tourists are often regarded as walking ATM machines. Due to their colonial past and present European immigration policies, Moroccans may also see Europeans, particularly the French and Spanish, as racist. Though they are quick to recognize the sophistication of such countries, Moroccans also tend to view most Westerners as naive. If you live in the same place for some time, however, this perception soon disappears. When people realize you are there to stay, you will be welcomed as "one of the family."

Moroccans are generally infatuated with Western culture, as is apparent from the

American and European pop music competing with the *muezzin* (proclaimer of the call to prayer) to the knockoff Burberry, Dolce & Gabbana, and Armani clothing worn by urban sophisticates. And while many Moroccans disagree with certain Western policies, the vast majority are able to separate the government from the people and will not blame you, the foreigner, for the actions of your country.

Attitudes toward other Arabs are difficult to pinpoint—some Moroccans are jealous of the wealth of countries like the UAE, others are disdainful of the illiberal way women in certain societies are treated. There is, of course, a kinship with other Muslims, regardless of nationality; however, most Moroccans are above all proud of their national heritage.

Unfortunately, there is one group of people who suffer the disadvantages of an inferior status in Moroccan society. Sub-Saharan Africans often come to Morocco in search of a better life or as a stopover in their attempts to reach Europe. Whether it is because they often manage to find work (thus "taking" jobs from Moroccans) or because of their skin color (despite Morocco's great mixture of skin tones, lighter is still "better"), they are looked down on by Moroccans. Recently, the Moroccan police appeared to confirm this prejudice when, in cahoots with the Spanish government, they dumped a large number of sub-Saharan Africans in the desert without food or water after they had been arrested for attempting to cross the borders to Ceuta and Melilla illegally.

An interesting phenomenon that occurs with foreign employees, particularly teachers who work closely with Moroccan youth, is that of instant celebrity—it can be difficult to escape being approached on the street by young people who just want to practice your language with you. Fortunately, these encounters can generally be taken at face value, and may even result in you being taken out for coffee or, better yet, invited home for a meal.

WOMEN IN SOCIETY

The position of women in Moroccan society has been transformed over the past decade, and women's rights, access to education, attitudes, and other norms are still changing rapidly. Although there is still a vast divide between the cities and the countryside, the number of young women attending secondary school and university continues to rise, and progress is being made even in the remotest of places. Training schemes run by urban doctors and Peace Corps volunteers have increased awareness of prenatal and child health in the countryside, for example. Such programs have not only lowered the infant mortality rate but have also raised the status of rural women by training them in fields such as midwifery.

In Morocco as elsewhere, it is urban women who have the greatest opportunities. Most are able to finish school to baccalaureate level, and many go on to study at university. They have the right to marry whomever they choose, initiate divorce proceedings, and run for public office. As a result of unprecedented changes to the *Moudawana* (Family Law) introduced by King Mohammed VI in 2004, women enjoy equal rights with men in the areas of marriage, divorce, and the custody of children (though it is worth noting that polygamy is still legal, but only with the permission of the first wife). Women in Morocco can and do wear what they like, which includes choosing whether or not to wear the *hijab*, the traditional Muslim head scarf—not to be confused with the *niqaab*, which veils the whole face and is rarely seen in Morocco, except among older women and the poor. Women are now frequently seen in cafés even in smaller cities, though usually on the second floor, away from the stares of passing men.

Of course, Rome wasn't built in a day, and Moroccan women still have a ways to go. They can smoke in public, but those who do are often shunned. Being seen in a bar or hotel is *hshuma* and even dating before marriage is viewed with suspicion, as Muslim girls are expected to remain virgins until their wedding day. Nevertheless, many young Moroccans engage in romantic relationships, though mostly of the innocent variety, involving incessant phone calls and SMS messages. Abandonment of wives is still commonplace, and girls who get pregnant out of wedlock are either kicked out of their homes, forced to marry quickly, or face the shame of going to Casablanca for an abortion (which is strictly forbidden by Islam).

Foreign women are, generally speaking, placed outside these parameters; they will rarely receive a second glance for smoking in public, for example, something that would invite considerable *hshuma* for a Moroccan. And though it is important to dress modestly and respect the culture, foreign women are relatively free to do what they wish.

The fact that Moroccan women are often better off than their Muslim counterparts elsewhere is due to their own struggle for equal rights as well as a sympathetic and progressive king. And as long as feminists like Fatima Mernissi, author of *Beyond the Veil* among other scholarly works, continue the fight, Moroccan women can only march forward.

SEXUAL MORES

In Moroccan society the only legitimate sexual relations are those within a legal marriage. A female who has not yet married—and thus lost her virginity—is called a *bint* (girl), whereas one who has married is a *mar'a* (woman). As we have seen, 70 percent of Morocco's population are under thirty, so despite the ideal of virginity, young men rarely approach marriage without some sexual experience. Much of this comes from prostitutes, who are widely tolerated though their profession is not legal. Homosexual relations between adolescent boys are not uncommon either, especially in the conservative countryside where boys and girls are often separated from adolescence until marriage.

An increasing number of young women are now sexually active as well; unfortunately this is not a step forward for Moroccan women. Religious values aside, sex education is lacking and most sexual encounters between young men and women involve unprotected sex. In addition, many young women, in an attempt to protect their "virginity" for marriage, engage in other sexual activities that can be just as dangerous in terms of sexually transmitted diseases.

Homosexual acts are forbidden in Islam; however, homosexual prostitution is common though most patrons are foreign men. Lesbianism is mostly unheard of, and homosexual relations in general are thought to be degrading. The Moroccan word for gay is *zamel* ("to mount") and is highly offensive. Morocco doesn't have a "gay community," though with the advent of the Internet, there are several Web sites catering to gay Moroccans—in practice, many of these are used to meet foreigners who pay for sexual services.

Sex tourism is prevalent. Europeans and Middle Easterners in particular travel to Morocco looking for an exotic experience, and patronize both prostitutes and single Moroccans. Moroccan men, on the other hand, may turn to foreign women for sex or marriage (which would enable them to emigrate). This is an area that can lead to misunderstanding and mistrust. Foreigners should respect the norms, be aware of religious values, and refrain from inappropriate behavior that could lead to misunderstanding.

Despite these warnings, there are plenty of successful relationships between foreigners and Moroccans—it is simply important to be cautious when entering into one. Meet the friends and family of your new acquaintance and, if possible, introduce your friends and family as well. As with all relationships, follow your instincts.

chapter three

BELIEFS, TRADITIONS, & CELEBRATIONS

NATIONAL HOLIDAYS

Morocco has several national holidays during which banks, public offices, schools, and most shops close. As Morocco officially follows the Western Gregorian calendar, the nonreligious holidays fall on fixed dates each year. Though there are often street celebrations, these holidays are not of great importance to most Moroccans, unlike the religious holidays. However, many people take the opportunity to visit family and then public transportation can be packed.

New Year's Day: January 1

This is not an important holiday for most Moroccans, as the Islamic New Year falls at a different time; however, it is celebrated, particularly in the Atlantic coastal cities, with a special dinner, a party, and plenty of delicious confections. Cities such as Rabat and Marrakech are beginning to hold public celebrations similar to those found in Europe and the U.S.A.

Independence Manifesto: January 11

This commemorates the Istiqlal Party's issuing of the "Independence Manifesto" in 1944, which demanded recognition of Morocco's independence, its territorial integrity, and its national sovereignty as embodied by King Mohammed V.

Labor Day: May 1

As in many other countries around the world, Labor Day is celebrated on May 1.

Feast of the Throne: July 30

July 30 marks the accession to the throne of His Majesty King Mohammed VI.

Allegiance of Oued Ed-Dahab: August 14

This occasion commemorates the 1979 pledge of allegiance by leaders of the Oued Ed-Dahab (Dakhla) province to Morocco, renouncing the Polisario's claim on their territory.

Anniversary of the King's and People's Revolution: August 20

This day commemorates the 1953 enforced exile of Mohammed V; his "sacrificing" of the throne triggered a revolution.

Young People's Day: August 21

This celebrates the present king's birthday.

Anniversary of the Green March: November 6

Known as *Eid al-Massira al-Khedra* in Arabic and *La Marche Verte* in French, this holiday commemorates the 1975 march of over three hundred and fifty thousand Moroccans into the Western Sahara to "reclaim" it for Morocco. Led by Hassan II, the march sparked a new wave of Moroccan patriotism.

Independence Day: November 18

This holiday commemorates Morocco's independence, granted by the French on November 18, 1956, and the return of King Mohammed V to the throne. The year 2006 commemorated the fiftieth anniversary of Moroccan independence with spectacular celebrations.

RELIGIOUS HOLIDAYS

The Islamic, or *Hijra*, calendar is lunar-based; therefore the Islamic year is about eleven days shorter than the Western Gregorian one. The word *Hijra* describes the Prophet Mohammed's journey from Mecca to Medina in 622 CE, thus marking the first year of the *Hijra* calendar, or 1 AH (Latin for *Anno Hegirae*).

Although Moroccan calendars and date books provide official dates for these holidays in advance, they are not actually determined until the new moon is sighted, and confirmed by the religious authorities in Fès. Moroccans will often claim to know the date on which *Ramadan* begins or ends, but in practice, everyone waits, if necessary, until the last minute when the mosques and television give the proper announcements.

Ras as-Sana
Meaning "head of the year," this is the Islamic New Year and is celebrated on 1 *Moharram*, the first day of the first month of the *Hijra* calendar.

Ashora
Although Morocco is a Sunni Muslim country, it also celebrates this Shiite holy day, on 10 *Moharram*, commemorating the assassination of Hussein Ibn Ali, the grandson of the Prophet Mohammed. Children are given candies and toys.

Moulid an-Nabi
This holiday, on 12 *Rabi al-Awal*, the third month of the *Hijra* calendar, celebrates the birthday of the Prophet Mohammed.

Ramadan
Ramadan, the ninth month of the *Hijra* calendar, is the month in which the Qur'an was first

revealed. It is a period of fasting (*sawm*), during which Muslims are expected to abstain from eating, drinking, smoking, and sex from dawn until dusk. The spiritual benefits of the fast are nullified by lying or by talking about someone behind their back. A *hadith* recommends that women dress conservatively and modestly without ornamentation during this time, and most women abide by this until sundown. Children and the elderly are not expected to fast and women who are pregnant, lactating, or menstruating and anyone who is traveling or ill are exempt, though the days missed must be made up later in the year.

Ramadan is taken quite seriously in Morocco, and Muslims can be arrested for eating on the street during this time, but it is quite common (particularly for young people) to sneak food in private. Non-Muslim foreigners are not required to fast, though they should be discreet. Discretion isn't much of a problem as most restaurants and cafés are closed until dusk, and some close for the entire month, using the time for renovations.

The fast is broken at dusk, when one cannot "distinguish a white thread from a black thread" in the hand. It is not necessary to perform this test, however, as in most cities a cannon is fired that can be heard for miles. In some smaller towns this act is performed by a trumpeter instead.

Television is also a good source of information, broadcasting both the prayer times and the time for *al-ftour*, or the breaking of the fast.

Al-ftour is a light meal, and though the content varies throughout the Islamic world, a date is generally eaten first everywhere, as that is how the Prophet Mohammed broke the fast. Following the dates, Moroccans partake of *harira*, a delicious tomato-based soup that can be vegetarian or made with meat; *shebakia*, a sickly-sweet pastry that never seems to spoil; milk; and various pastries made at home or purchased at a café (most of which convert their interiors into pastry shops during *Ramadan*) or a patisserie.

After *al-ftour*, there is plenty of socializing either at home, in cafés, or on the street. The next meal is essentially dinner, and is generally more lavish than during the rest of the year. It is eaten between 10:00 p.m. and 1:00 a.m. and is followed by a brief nap. About two hours before dawn, another cannon shot signals that it is time to eat again. During this final meal, called *suhoor*, Muslims will take in enough food and water to last the whole day.

Last but not least, the twenty-seventh night of *Ramadan*, or *lilt al-Qader* (the "night of Power"), is a particularly holy night during which the Qur'an is read in its entirety at the mosque. Many devout Muslims spend the whole night in prayer, taking breaks to eat or nap if necessary. A person who dies on this night is said to gain immediate entrance to Paradise.

Breakfast Feast (*Eid al-Fitr*)

Eid al-Fitr, also called *Eid al-Seghir* or "Little Feast," signifies the end of *Ramadan*. On the day before the holiday, the shops and patisseries are crowded with people buying last-minute gifts and sweets for the festivities. Children receive new clothes, and people travel far and wide to visit family. The holiday usually lasts for three days, during which time most shops are closed, except in cities where tourism is the major industry, and there is a general festive air that is reminiscent of Christmas. It is not uncommon for white-collar employees to receive a small bonus at this time.

The Great Feast (*Eid al-Adha,* or *Eid al-Kabir*)

The last month of the Islamic calendar, *Zuul-Hijja*, is when the *hajj*, or pilgrimage to Mecca, is undertaken. The *hajj* culminates in the ritual slaughter of a lamb to commemorate the offering by Ibrahim (Abraham) of a ram instead of his son. This ritual is replicated by every family that can afford to buy a lamb on *Eid al-Adha*. The holiday lasts for three days, from 10 to 13 *Zuul-Hijja*, and like most Moroccan holidays is a time for families to feast and spend time together.

MOUSSEMS

A *moussem* is the commemoration of the anniversary of the birth or death of a saint, called a *murabit*. At this time, some Moroccans may perform a brief pilgrimage to the site where the *moussem* festivities take place. Although the veneration of saints is forbidden by Islam, these festivals are a part of Moroccan culture and are inspired by a mix of Islamic and other traditions.

During a *moussem*, there is music and dancing and general revelry. In the south, *gnaoua*

 musicians (dancer-musicians descended from sub-Saharan Africans who live in the south) may perform. A *moussem* is also a good opportunity to see a *fantasia*, during which a group of horsemen in traditional garb line up at opposite ends of a field, charge toward one another, and shoot their rifles into the air. Though this was once traditional in Morocco, it is now done for the sake of tourists and to celebrate the *moussem*.

Popular *moussems* include the *Moussem* Moulay Abdallah in El Jadida in October and the *Moussem* Moulay Idriss in Meknes and Moulay Idriss Zerhoun.

FESTIVALS AND CELEBRATIONS

Morocco has secular and cultural festivals that attract Moroccans and tourists alike; some are quite traditional and others are more modern, but none should be missed!

Almond Blossom Festival (February)
This festival commemorates the beginning of the spring blossom season and is held in the Ameln Valley near Tafraoute.

Marathon des Sables (March/April)
A seven-day footrace through the desert that starts and ends in Ouarzazate.

Rose Festival (May)
This festival celebrates the harvest of roses in the valley of El Kelaa des M'Gouna, near Ouarzazate.

Festival of World Sacred Music (May/June/July)
A nine-day festival drawing international visitors, the World Sacred Music Festival is held in Fès in the early summer months.

Cherry Festival (June)
Held in Sefrou, this festival lasts three days and has plenty of music and dancing. It ends in the crowning of the Cherry Queen.

National Folklore Festival (June)
A festival celebrating Berber music and dance, the National Folklore Festival is held in Marrakech.

***Gnaoua* and World Music Festival** (June)
Arguably Morocco's most popular festival, this celebration of world music draws thousands of visitors to the small port town of Essaouira. In 2004 the Wailers (of Bob Marley and the Wailers fame) performed, drawing record numbers of international tourists.

Festival International de Rabat (June/July)
This festival draws musicians from all over Africa and is also the setting for a small film festival.

International Cultural Festival (July/August)
This arts festival is held in Asilah, a small port town. It celebrates both contemporary art and traditional Moroccan art and is very family-friendly.

Marriage Festival (September)
This three-day festival is held in Imilchil and has been highly exploited in recent years by the Moroccan National Tourist Office. During the festival, young Berber women choose prospective husbands and sign papers of engagement.

International Film Festival (varies)
Drawing international artists, directors, and
actors, this film festival is held in Marrakech and
has become something of an elite event. It lasts
one week and showcases Arab and African films,
as well as others.

FOLKLORE AND MYSTICISM

Though Morocco is a Muslim country, its history
goes back thousands of years before the arrival
of Islam, a fact that is reflected in certain
practices. In the early days of Islam, some
believers didn't find living by the rules of
religion to be enough, and sought a closer
relationship with God. Called Sufis, many of
these spiritual seekers found a connection with
the early practices of the Berbers. There are still
some Sufis in Morocco, particularly in the south,
where they live in *zawiyas*, or Sufi brotherhoods.

Though Sufis are a small minority, certain
mystical or superstitious practices are
popular with the vast majority of
Moroccans. There is a strong belief in the
evil eye, and an amulet known as the
Hand of Fatima (or *hamza* in Jewish
folklore) is often worn around the
neck or hung above the doorway.
Facial tattoos are still applied in certain

parts of the southern countryside, and are thought to ward off evil spirits, called *djinns*. Aisha Qandisha is one such creature: a beautiful woman with the legs of a goat, she is thought to live in rivers or even in drainpipes. Children are frightened of her and Moroccan men have been known to fall under her spell.

There are other less-known folkloric practices, but these are virtually unheard of in the cities, where modern Moroccans will denounce them as un-Islamic. During the myriad festivals and *moussems* that take place during the year, it is possible for foreigners to see—or even take part in—a host of Moroccan folkloric traditions.

chapter four

MAKING FRIENDS

Making friends in Morocco is seemingly easy—Moroccans love to talk, and will want to make you feel welcome, particularly if you are alone in their country. It is maintaining friendships in Morocco that is often difficult, but there are a few common courtesies that will help you out along the way.

THE GENDER DIVIDE

If you arrive in Morocco as half of a married couple, making friends shouldn't prove too difficult. You will probably have plenty of coworkers or business associates who are also married and can anticipate your needs and help you out without any concerns about propriety.

It is the single foreigner who will struggle to understand the gender dynamics in Moroccan friendships. Traditionally in Islam, men and women are either strictly segregated or not accustomed to having friends of the opposite sex. Though this is beginning to change, particularly with the youngest generation, certain gender rules apply; although foreigners are partially exempt, it's important to be aware of them.

Foreign men will find no trouble making friends with Moroccan men, particularly if they speak French (or Arabic, of course). If you are single, you will often be invited out for coffee, or even for drinks—it is typical for the host to pay, and though you should offer to pay your share, it will most likely be refused. When you invite a friend, however, you can repay the kindness by picking up the tab. Moroccan men are often quite affectionate with one another, and an arm around the shoulder or even hand-holding is perfectly normal heterosexual behavior. Age is not important in Moroccan friendships—it is common to see young and older men spending time together.

Where problems arise is in friendships between foreign men and Moroccan women. As the latter do not usually have Moroccan male friends, they may also be hesitant about befriending a male foreigner. If a female friend or colleague does issue an invitation to meet her family at home, the male visitor will often spend the whole time with her male family members.

Foreign women, on the other hand, have the best of both worlds. They can more easily befriend Moroccan women, and will have men jostling to get their phone number. In a culture where men and women are supposed to keep apart, a foreign woman can be quite an exciting prospect for a Moroccan man. The problem lies in deciphering *why*—he may genuinely want your friendship to gain a woman's perspective or simply because he finds you interesting. He may also believe the stereotype that foreign women are "loose" or "easy," or he may be looking for a way out of the country. Trust your instincts. Moroccans are naturally curious, so his motive may be honorable, but it pays to be cautious.

FORMS OF ADDRESS

Men are typically referred to as *sidi*, the Arabic equivalent of "mister." It is sometimes shortened to *si*. If you want to get the attention of a man you don't know, it's acceptable to simply call him *sidi*. It is also common, when dealing with servers, to call them "Sidi Mohammed." The title *moulay* is also used for men, but generally only in reference to holy men, living or departed. Occasionally a professor or lawyer will proclaim himself a *moulay*. *Hajj* is used as a title for those who have completed the *hajj*, or sometimes for the elderly. *Hajja* is the female equivalent. For other women, *lalla* is the common prefix, and can be used like *sidi* in order to attract a woman's attention.

KEEPING IN TOUCH

In dealing with new friends or even business contacts, it is common courtesy to phone often or send SMS messages, which are extremely popular and, incidentally, cheaper. It is customary to inquire about the health and family of your friend. Greetings are formalized and standard, and are addressed further in Chapter 9. It is extremely important to learn the standard forms of address, as insufficient greetings can damage a budding friendship in ways that are difficult to comprehend or repair.

There is an interesting phenomenon with cell phones—a Moroccan may call a friend and hang up, registering their own number on their friend's phone. Called a *beep aliyah* among young people, this is just a way of letting someone know you're thinking about them—a return call is not necessary, just send a *beep aliyah* their way. This method of keeping in touch is probably so popular because calls from Moroccan cell phones are free if no one answers.

HOSPITALITY AND INVITATIONS HOME

Moroccans are well-known for their extraordinary hospitality; you may receive an invitation to lunch before your host even knows your name! Don't feel obligated to accept, as the inviting party will probably not be offended if you decline. If a friend is inviting you home, however, he or she probably really means it. Generally speaking, any invitation from a new friend to visit their home is for lunch (or dinner) and a meal should be expected. Rarely will a Moroccan ask you to find their house—usually, you will be picked up or a common meeting place will be set. It is polite—but not obligatory—to bring a small gift. Dates, a sugar cone, or anything from your own culture is appropriate.

When you arrive at the home, it is customary to remove your shoes at the door. If you are being entertained by a coworker or employer, you will most likely be led to the *bet diyaf*, or guest room. More intimate friends will invite you directly into their sitting room, where the family usually eats. In very traditional households, and particularly if you are a man, there may not be any women present during the meal, but this is becoming less and less common in the cities.

Once seated, you will be served coffee, tea, or milk, sometimes accompanied by dates. The television may be turned on (and tuned in to an English-language channel) or you may sit and chat. After some time, it is not impolite to mention food or that you are hungry, signaling that the meal can begin.

The diners will first wash their hands. Sometimes this is done at the sink; at other times the more traditional method is used—a kettle and basin are passed around for washing one's hands. When it is brought to you, you should hold your hands over the basin while your host pours the water, and use the soap provided. You will then be given a towel to dry your hands.

Moroccans usually eat at a low, round table out of a common dish. Utensils may be used, or smaller dishes handed out for distributing individual portions. Traditionally, Moroccans eat with their hands or a piece of bread, which is used to scoop or soak up the food. Eat only from the section of the dish, or *tajine*, directly in front of you (using your right hand, of course: see more  on page 153)—it is considered rude to reach across to someone else's portion. Your host may select the best cuts of meat and place them in your section—this sometimes includes bits such as the liver or heart of the chicken. If a selection is placed in front of you that you absolutely cannot stomach, take care not to express your disgust: just apologize and explain that it's something you're not accustomed to eating.

Moroccans love to ensure that their guests are well fed. Unfortunately, "well fed" can mean "stuffed to the gills." Moroccan mothers in particular are known for chanting *"Kul! Kul!"* at their guests, which means "Eat! Eat!" Your best bet is to acquiesce, but if you absolutely can't manage another mouthful, apologize and say *"Ana la akulu katheeran,"* which means "I don't eat much." This will reassure your hosts that the problem lies with your appetite and not their food.

At the end of the main course, fresh seasonal fruit is usually served, followed by mint tea. It is appropriate at any time to praise the food and your host, and burping, followed by thanks to God (*"alhamdulillah"*), is perfectly acceptable.

After the meal, it is polite to linger for some time—Moroccans would never think of asking a guest to leave, and after a meal you will often be invited to join your hosts in a brief nap. If you must leave, you will find yourself having to repeat this several times to your host, and you should expect to be met with protests. It's a good idea to inform your host in advance if you have a later appointment at a specific time.

FITTING IN
Morocco is not an easy place to simply "fit in." Unless you look Moroccan or speak *derija*

fluently, there is virtually no way you'll be able to avoid standing out. That said, by increasing your awareness of the cultural norms and practices, you will be able to get to know Morocco and its people on a deeper level.

Even if you have not studied Arabic formally, making an effort to learn the alphabet and some key phrases goes further than you might think. Unlike the French, who would rather you speak English than butcher their language, Moroccans take kindly to hearing foreigners' attempts to speak Arabic. Although you may be corrected frequently, your efforts will be appreciated.

Dressing modestly is important, particularly for women. Keep in mind, however, that modest does not necessarily mean conservative. Even women who wear the *hijab* are often at the forefront of fashion; it is quite possible to preserve your own sense of style while keeping covered up. Tattoos are considered *haram* (forbidden in Islam) and should be covered up. Small body piercings (e.g., nose rings) are uncommon but not forbidden and are acceptable in foreigners so long as they are fairly discreet.

The best way to fit into Moroccan society is simply to be yourself. Although individuality is not a particularly prized asset, authenticity is. If you are genuine, open, and respectful, you will fit in with your Moroccan friends just fine.

DAILY LIFE

SOCIAL STRUCTURE

The importance of family in Moroccan life is evident in the language—Arabic contains different sets of words to describe specific family members. For example, the word for maternal aunt (*khala*) is different from paternal aunt (*'ama*) and explaining one's distant relatives can be quite complicated.

Traditionally, men are honored before women; this can be frustrating for foreign women who find, when out and about with male friends, that they are often completely ignored.

Family takes precedence at all times. Most Moroccans would never dream of marrying

without their parents' permission (though legally they can do so at eighteen) and young people do not aspire to move out of the family home until they are married. A typical household consists of a married couple, their children, and their elderly parents or unwed brothers and sisters. Moroccans look down on societies that abandon the aged in nursing homes.

Individualism is only now becoming prevalent among the youngest generation, as is apparent in their clothing and sometimes their attitudes. Moroccans outside this generation tend to conform; whether due to the prevailing sense of fatalism or a fear of authority, the majority would never dream of straying from the fold.

DRESS

There is not one statement that can be made about dress in Morocco that would uniformly apply to all Moroccans. Clothing varies according to class, personal taste, and specific demand, which is to say most people have occasion to wear modern and traditional clothes and probably own a good number of both.

Casual European or American-style clothes are the norm among the under-thirty crowd, and vary in quality. Morocco, possibly the designer knockoff capital of the world, is full of fake designer wares—after a while, you will notice that almost every girl is wearing Chanel sunglasses. Ironically, these items are often the cheapest.

The quintessential Moroccan garment is the *djellaba*, an ankle-length hooded robe with buttons up the front, worn by both men and women. *Djellabas* come in a range of fabrics. Most men wear either a white, off-white, or black one, which can be purchased "off-the-rack" or tailor-made. Women's *djellabas* range from very plain to very ornate, and everywhere in between, and since most women select the fabric and have theirs tailor-made, you will even spot *djellabas* made from faux fur, plaid, or even leopard print. Another traditional garment is the *caftan* (an ornate and flowing robe), which is worn only for more formal or special occasions.

A stroll through the public square of any city is enough to see the importance of shoes—it is difficult for a man to walk a few yards without

being accosted by a shoeshine boy! Moroccan men are very particular about having clean, well-shined shoes, and even sneakers are well-kempt. Moroccan women, even those dressed in *djellaba* and *hijab*, often choose to wear heels.

Moroccans rarely wear shoes inside the home, where another type of shoe, the *bilgha*, is used. These backless leather slippers come in a variety of shapes and colors and are worn around the house and outdoors (a recent innovation is an "all-terrain" rubber sole). The men's classic style is yellow and pointy-toed while women can choose from an array of colors and designs.

Personal Ornamentation

Although cosmetics and jewelry are just as common in Morocco as everywhere else, an excess of either is not appropriate. Gold is considered a token of wealth and is worn by both genders despite the fact that the Qur'an forbids it for men. Berber jewelry is more commonly made of silver, and is popular with Moroccans and tourists alike.

At some point, you will inevitably see an older woman with facial tattoos—traditionally, Berber women were given permanent tattoos on their cheeks, foreheads, and chins. These were used both for tribal identification and to ward off spirits. While most women who sport these tattoos are elderly, you will occasionally see a younger woman with them in the countryside. Tattooing is prohibited by Islam, but is an example of how earlier cultural traditions have coexisted with religion in Morocco.

Moroccan Headwear

Though baseball caps and hats fashionable elsewhere in the world are also popular in

Morocco, there are a few traditional pieces of headwear worth mentioning. The fez, or *tarboosh*, is a round felt hat with a flat top and no brim that now seems to be disappearing. It is mainly a ceremonial hat, worn by officials and by the King in many public portraits. Its origins are unclear, but in the nineteenth century it became popular elsewhere under Ottoman rule. The name is thought to derive from the city of Fès, where the signature crimson dye was made. In much of the Muslim world, the fez is now considered the headwear of the oppressors (the Ottoman Turks).

Turbans are mostly worn by rural men (with colors denoting tribal affiliations). Skullcaps, slightly flattened on the top, are usually associated with fundamentalist men (who are also easily spotted by their beards, often minus a mustache) but others may also have occasion to wear them.

The most important and noticeable piece of headwear, however, is worn by women. The *hijab*, an item of controversy around the world, is considered compulsory by many Muslim women. Some interpret the Qur'an as requiring women to cover their heads while others believe it is necessary only to be modest. Either way, the *hijab* is respected in Morocco, even by those who do not aspire to wear it. Generally speaking, it is a scarf that covers the hair, ears, and neck. While some Moroccan women may cover their hair with a scarf from time to time, a *hijabi* will always wear her scarf past the hairline and pinned tightly on her head. She will also dress modestly, usually covering her bottom with a long shirt or skirt, sometimes even over jeans.

In Morocco, it is entirely up to a girl, and sometimes her family, whether or not she chooses to wear the *hijab*. Most girls who decide to wear it begin in their mid-teens, though some women don't put it on until marriage. Generally speaking, once someone starts to wear the *hijab*, she will continue to do so.

BARGAINING—A WAY OF LIFE

Bargaining is truly a way of life in Morocco. Europeans and Americans are often surprised to see that everything—well, just about everything— is up for negotiation, from carrots to cell phones to clothing. For Moroccans, bargaining is an art form, a game, and a means of social interaction. And if buyers feel that they got ripped off, it is their own fault for not bargaining successfully! It's important to learn a few rules of bargaining to ensure that you're getting a good deal.

When a Moroccan shopkeeper sees a tourist heading his way, his first thought is that he's going to make a sale. It's important not to show too much interest, particularly in the item you *really* want—instead, show interest in another, less expensive item to get an idea of the prices. Using Arabic will go a long way, as will talking about your profession or what you're doing in Morocco. Foreign residents, though still considered wealthier than the average Moroccan, are often quoted better prices than tourists and can sometimes walk away with the "Moroccan price."

After you've been quoted a price on the lesser item, look around a bit more, then casually ask the price of the item you really want. You will probably be quoted around two to three times the amount the shopkeeper will actually accept. Don't be dismayed—this is simply the opening offer. Depending on your opinion of the item's quality, counter with one-third to one-half of the quoted figure. The shopkeeper will likely balk, comment on your frugality, and maybe even call you Berber (Berbers are known as hard bargainers). Unless you have gravely insulted him, he will probably lower the price just a little—counter his offer by upping yours a bit. This process can go back and forth many times; when you get close to what the shopkeeper will sell it for, he'll probably ask for your "best price." You can either choose to give him your true best price, or one that's slightly below it, but be prepared to reach an agreement. Even before you shake hands on the deal, he may begin to package the item, securing the purchase for himself. This is a good time to throw in your absolute last offer, and he will do the same. The sale ends in a shaking of hands, and perhaps a cup of mint tea, if the purchase is a large one.

Bargaining is expected when shopping for souvenirs, housewares, and clothing. It is also possible to bargain at food markets, but generally the price will only come down if you buy in volume. Prices are generally fixed when labeled as such, but it's always worth asking.

It pays to make friends with merchants—they will often honor return customers with excellent prices, and most have friends who deal in other products, which can make your life a lot easier when you're looking for that one special item.

Try not to get too upset if you feel that you're being taken advantage of. Foreigners living in Morocco often feel entitled to Moroccan prices, and there are certainly ways of getting close (such as making friends with merchants and shopping with Moroccan friends), but to most Moroccans, a foreigner is at least on a par with the Moroccan middle class; therefore, they see no reason to give you the deal of a lifetime. It may just be easier to accept that your lifestyle costs a little more to maintain, as many middle-class Moroccans do.

STANDARDS OF LIVING

There are two distinct styles of housing in urban Morocco—*medina* houses and *ville nouvelle* apartments or villas. The vast majority of foreigners choose the latter, usually out of convenience. The major difference between the two is that *medina* homes often lack Western conveniences. Note that neither usually comes furnished, or with appliances.

A typical *medina* home is behind a large, nondescript door. Inside could be either a sumptuous palace or a modest den; either way, it is likely to be one or two floors, asymmetrical, and without many modern conveniences. Generally speaking, a house in the *medina* contains a squat or Turkish toilet, and may not have stable plumbing. An apartment in the *ville nouvelle* of a city is usually quite large, with several rooms for use as sitting rooms or bedrooms. It may or may not contain built-in closets (not traditional in Moroccan homes), and it is likely to have a Western toilet and regular bathtub or shower.

Much importance is placed on hospitality. Moroccan families usually have a formal room for entertaining guests that otherwise remains unused. Another room houses the TV and is used by family; if you are a close friend, you will usually be invited into this room for meals.

In rural areas, it is a different story—depending on the status and wealth of the family, a rural home could have just one or two rooms or several. Rural houses are usually made from mud brick or clay and are furnished similarly to urban homes, with banquettes or simply cushions.

Furnishing and Appliances

It would not be a stretch to suggest that every Moroccan home has a TV and satellite dish. Beyond that, it is a draw as to what other appliances may be in use. Moroccan families own either a three-ring or a full-sized gas stove for cooking. They will often have a hot water heater that is also hooked up to gas, a refrigerator, and a small washing machine. Anything else can be bought, however, as everything from hair dryers to flat-screen televisions is available in both name-brand and imitation form.

Moroccan homes are typically furnished rather homogenously; banquettes are built to fit the perimeter of the rooms, with low tables in the center for eating. In more traditional households, there are no rooms designated specifically as bedrooms; rather, the banquettes are used for both sitting and sleeping. Moroccan rugs, or *kilims*, are used generously to cover the floor.

Moroccans traditionally don't have designated bedrooms; generally, they will sleep in whichever room is furnished with banquettes. Many city dwellers have bedrooms, however, and beds are available both made-to-order in the *souqs* (markets) and in furniture stores. Though rooms tend not to have built-in closets, wardrobes and dressers are sold in the *souqs*.

DAILY LIFE AND ROUTINE

Moroccan society is changing fast and gender roles are become more relaxed, at least in the cities. Traditionally, men are wholly responsible for the protection and care of their family; this is evident from the fact that they rarely marry until they have a stable job and house. Women are conventionally responsible for the family and home, including the cooking, cleaning, and even partly the education of the children.

Daily life is relatively home-centered; parents and children generally return home for lunch, and entertaining within the home is the norm. During the summer in particular, people hardly seem to sleep; it is quite common to see entire families strolling outdoors at 11:00 p.m. and young men tend to stay out all night. The typical day starts somewhere between 6:00 and 8:00 a.m., and by 9:00 the streets and *medinas* are crowded.

Many modern Moroccan women have benefited from access to education, and are choosing to work. That said, a Moroccan woman's domain is still the home, and whatever her job, she tends to be very house-proud. Rooms in a Moroccan home are sparsely furnished and have tiled floors, making cleaning an easy task; buckets of water mixed with bleach and soap are dumped on the bare floor, which is scrubbed with a broom, then cleared with a squeegee.

Urban Life

Morocco's cities are expanding rapidly as rural migrants look for greater opportunities. Even in the smaller cities, new Western-style supermarkets are opening, expensive apartment buildings are being built, and new cinemas and other entertainment complexes are catering to the needs of the young and sophisticated generation.

Foreigners tend to live in cities, and urban Moroccans have become quite accustomed to this. In addition to the Western supermarkets cropping up around the country, cities have long catered to foreigners with smaller *épiceries* (groceries) selling goods such as pet food and

peanut butter that aren't native to Morocco. Each larger city also has an Institut Français, which provides both French-language classes and cultural events.

The metropolis of Casablanca in particular has seen an influx of migrants who have set up slums, or *bidonvilles*, outside the cities; built during the night in order to avoid the wrath of the police, these homes are intended as temporary refuges but often end up as permanent structures. Other smaller cities, particularly those popular with tourists, have also seen the growth of *bidonvilles*.

Rural Life

The *bled*, or countryside, particularly in the impoverished south, is quite a contrast to the hustle and bustle of the cities. Here, despite the ubiquitous rooftop satellite dishes, life has not changed in generations. Villages are sustained by the land, and many families have members who have left for the big city and send money home.

In general, Berber dialects are still the lingua franca of the *bled*, and most people identify themselves as Berber. It is rare to find women who have been educated beyond primary school, and arranged marriages are quite common; the village of Imilchil holds an annual festival where unmarried men and women are introduced and allowed to choose a partner, then quickly engaged.

Rural families, while initially wary of foreigners, are hospitable and warm. If given the opportunity to stay with one, don't miss it. People in the *bled* are considerably more superstitious than their urban counterparts, however, so ask before taking photographs.

BANKING

The Moroccan system of banking, based on the French system, has improved greatly in recent years. Bank al-Maghrib (Bank of Morocco) is government-controlled and therefore the only bank to issue currency. There are more than twenty commercial banks to choose from. Foreign residents may open a personal bank account; this process will require a variety of documents, the list of which is ever-changing, but will certainly include your *carte de séjour* (residence permit), your passport, and a copy of the lease to your home or apartment as proof of residence. It is important to consult a bank manager early on if you want to set up an account.

LIVING ALONE

To Moroccans, the concept of living alone is completely alien; the only Moroccans living alone are bachelor males who are sufficiently well-off to do so or who have to live away from family for work, and occasionally the elderly. Therefore, if you find yourself in this situation, you will become used to hearing the term *meskeen*, which means "poor thing." This can often be to your advantage, as hospitable Moroccans hate to see anyone forced to eat alone. After the meal, you may even be invited to spend the night, which of course you can gently decline if you feel uncomfortable. But make no mistake—any invitation extended by your host is heartfelt and genuine. Prepare to be invited home by coworkers, neighbors, even strangers; during *Ramadan* the invitations will only multiply.

BUREAUCRACY

The most annoying and unavoidable aspect of living in Morocco is the red tape, which must be endured to open bank accounts, sign work contracts, and gain residency as a foreigner.

Consult your prospective employer on specific requirements for your job, as these are ever-changing, but prepare by bringing an official copy of your university degree. Also, be sure to obtain official copies of everything you sign, including the lease to your apartment and your work contracts. Moroccans are used to this bureaucracy and will rarely indulge your complaints about it.

The attitude is one of *c'est la vie*. Moroccan officials can be brisk or welcoming—treat them with respect, and you will find them on your side.

Foreigners from most European and North American countries may stay for up to three months without a visa; after that, you must obtain your *carte de séjour*. Requirements for this permit change frequently, so it is best to visit the police in your town within a week of arriving to learn what they are. Work quickly to obtain the necessary papers, as Moroccan bureaucracy is slow-moving and exceptions are rarely made—if you don't, you may find yourself on a ferry to Spain.

In order to make certain documents official, the government requires the use of tax stamps, which come in various denominations and are sold at *tabacs* (tobacconists) and the post office. When submitting your papers for the *carte de séjour*, you will most likely require one tax stamp in a larger denomination for the application, and a 2dh tax stamp for every other paper you submit. Sometimes it is also necessary to have your papers certified at the city hall (*beladiya* in Arabic, *hôtel de ville* in French); this process is similar to notarization. Tax stamps may also be required for documents such as résumés, recommendations, and diplomas, to make them "official."

chapter six

TIME OUT

When you're faced with the hustle and bustle of Fès or Marrakech, Morocco may seem like a fast-paced country, but in fact Moroccans greatly value holidays, vacations, and long lunches, as this means that they are able to spend more time with their family. As family takes precedence over work, employers are usually quite generous with vacation days.

CAFÉ CULTURE

Every Moroccan village has at least one café. Moroccan cities, by contrast, seem to have more cafés than people! Based on the grand cafés of France, these are where men start and end their day, read the newspaper, sip their *café au lait* or *café normal*, snack on delectable pastries, and smoke countless cigarettes.

In the larger cities, today, there is a growing number of cafés that welcome women, and it is becoming less and less surprising to see women alone or even smoking.

When attending a café with Moroccan friends of either sex, be prepared to keep your money in your pocket. It is the duty of the host to pay for his or her guests, and some Moroccans will insist that, even if you are the one doing the inviting, you are still the guest. It would be rude to insist on paying and even ruder to try to sneakily hand money to the waiter. Coffee is cheap; it's best to just smile and say "*shukran*" (thank you)!

As alcohol is prohibited in Islam, any drinking is done surreptitiously. That said, larger cities are teeming with bars, and one only has to look for the Flag Spéciale or Stork beer logo above a windowless door. These rather seedy bars are the haunts of men, and any women inside are probably prostitutes. If you want a drink, however, there are plenty of hotels, most of which have pleasant bars where foreigners and Moroccans alike can drink. In cities, alcohol is readily available at supermarkets and small shops.

THE PROMENADE

After the work day ends and the sun begins to set, Moroccans take to the streets for an evening stroll. This is a time for both men and women to meet with friends, window-shop, and check out the opposite sex. In most cities, the wide streets of the *ville nouvelle* will be the most crowded, but the *medina* is also a nice place for a walk and as an added bonus, prices in shops are often lowest at this time as shopkeepers try to get in the last few sales of the day.

ENTERTAINMENT

If you will be staying in a big city, fear not, as there is plenty of entertainment to be found. Larger cities have an Institut Français, which offers cultural and musical events, and one has only to look at the sides of buildings to see flyers advertising other performances—hip hop in particular has hit Morocco, so if that's your thing, you'll find no shortage of live shows! Western high culture can be found mainly in Casablanca and Rabat, but Arabic and Moroccan music performances are found everywhere, from classical to *chaabi*, or Arabic pop music. Marrakech boasts the incredible Royal Theater, which, though new, is built to mirror the architecture of Marrakech's oldest buildings. The theater offers productions from Shakespeare to touring companies to Moroccan dance and music performances and even children's recitals.

Cinema

All Moroccan cities have at least one cinema, and the larger cities have plenty, many of which welcome men and women alike. Unfortunately, there is little for Anglophones, as most Hollywood films are now dubbed into French. Still, Hollywood blockbusters, Bollywood spectacles, and Moroccan films are all available at the cinema, which is quite cheap and can make for an enjoyable afternoon.

Television and DVDs

Fortunately for English-speakers, there is a wide variety of films available elsewhere. Satellite TV can be bought for a relatively low one-time price, and the hundreds of channels offered in a variety of languages make it worth the expense. The main Moroccan channel, 2M—as well as a number of European channels—shows Hollywood films in the original language. Other channels feature sitcoms, news, and sports in English. DVDs of films from around the world are cheap, widely available, and compatible with most systems.

Nightlife

Being a Muslim country, Morocco is not the first place most people go to for nightlife, and rightly so—outside the big cities, there isn't much. Smaller towns and villages seem to close down after 9:00 or 10:00 p.m. and women remaining out on the streets after that will receive unwanted attention. For those living in Casablanca, Rabat, or Marrakech, however, it's a different story. Foreigners living in smaller towns often travel to these cities for an escape from early nights. Here, there are typical Western-style nightclubs where foreigners and the Moroccan bourgeoisie alike dance the night away. Dress is usually quite formal; a tie may be required for men and jeans may be prohibited—even if they're not, you'll rarely see Moroccans wearing them, as they tend to put on their best clothes for these affairs. These spots typically play a variety of music, the most popular styles being techno, hip hop, and *chaabi*.

There are typical Western nightclubs and then there are "nightclubs"—smaller establishments generally patronized only by men. Found in all the big cities, they are often the only type of night spot in smaller places like Meknes. Some feature belly dancers—keep in mind that belly dancing is *not* native to Morocco; the dancers are often excellent, however. Generally speaking, any woman (aside from the dancer) found in these clubs is a prostitute or a foreigner. Prostitutes are usually quite discreet, dressing in regular Western-style clothes, so be wary of any Moroccan woman approaching you in this type of club.

FOOD AND DRINK

Moroccan cuisine is rich and varied, owing to a variety of cultural influences. Meat is well-spiced and lean, vegetables are fresh and abundant, and everything is permeated with spices. Moroccan cooking is quite labor-intensive and dishes are well presented as well as meticulously prepared.

Beef, lamb, and chicken are all popular and used in a variety of dishes. Pigeon is also available, and the seafood in the coastal cities is not to be missed. Meat is prepared according to Islamic *halal* regulations, which prohibit the consumption of pork products. Products derived from pig can only be found in the most touristy restaurants and Western-style supermarkets.

Rice and semolina grains (*couscous*, see below) are used for a variety of dishes, and produce is often seasonal and homegrown. A wide range of spices are used, including cumin, saffron, paprika, ginger, cinnamon, red and black pepper, and a special mixture called *ras al-hanout* (literally, "head of the shop").

A typical Moroccan meal starts with something small—olives or a salad of cooked vegetables and bread—and a cold beverage. The main course is then brought out, usually in a large pot, or *tajine*. Moroccans will either eat from the main dish with spoons or their hands, or serve food on to individual dishes. After the main course is through and plates are removed, various fruits are arranged on the table, and mint tea is served, sometimes with cookies.

Breakfast (*al-Ftour*)
Moroccan breakfasts are nothing short of delightful. Whether you're eating at someone's home or a café, you are likely to see the following:

Beghrir
A sort of pancake, *beghrir* is smooth on one side and full of little bubbles on the other. Made from semolina and wheat flour, these delectable treats are best served with honey or sugar.

Harsha
A thick, unleavened pancake made from semolina, *harsha* is best served with honey or cream cheese and is most delicious when hot. There are stands everywhere that sell *harsha*.

Melwi
Melwi is a simple flour-based pancake that can be served with honey or stuffed with onions and spices. It is often sold alongside *harsha*.

Petit Pain
A distinctly French treat, "*petit pain*" is used in Morocco to refer to most French pastries available

at breakfast. A typical *petit pain* is flaky and best served warm.

Marrakshia

Popular in the Middle Atlas region, the *marrakshia* is a chocolate-frosted, crème-filled, heavy pastry. Delicious and quite addictive.

Lunch and Dinner

Moroccans usually eat lunch at home. However, plenty of restaurants are open during this time to cater both to foreigners and locals who work and can't make it home for lunch. Lunch is the biggest meal of the day, and dinner is actually quite light.

Harira

A thick, spicy, tomato-based soup, *harira* contains noodles and chickpeas and whatever else is in season. It is served every day during *Ramadan* to break the fast, but can be found during the rest of the year as an appetizer or a late-night dinner.

Couscous

Quite possibly the Moroccan national dish, *couscous* is traditionally served on Fridays for lunch. The women in the household prepare the dish while the men are praying at the mosque, and then the family sits down to eat together. Moroccan *couscous* consists of semolina grains (known by the same name) topped with vegetables and meat. There are several variations, but the most common contains seven vegetables, mostly tubers and squash, and chicken, beef, or fish. Another popular *couscous* dish is cooked with chicken, cinnamon, and raisins.

Tajine

A *tajine* is a round earthenware cooking dish with a wide lip and conical lid. Any dish cooked in one, save for *couscous*, also goes by the name of *tajine*. A *tajine* is a thick stew, often tomato-based, and contains meat and different types of vegetables. One popular variation is made with tomatoes, *kefta* (spiced meatballs), and eggs. Another features lemons, chicken, and olives.

B'stela

B'stela, sometimes spelled *pastilla*, is a delicious sweet and savory dish. It is made of fine layers of pastry, stuffed with pigeon and almonds, and spiced with cinnamon and pepper. *B'stela* is usually served for special occasions, but can be ordered in advance from many restaurants.

Restaurants

Most Moroccans prefer to eat at home, with family. That said, there is no dearth of restaurants in the country—even the tiniest hamlet will have some sort of rest stop for those unable to make it home for lunch. Casablanca and Rabat are both filled with restaurants of just about every variety, from Senegalese to sushi to KFC. The other larger cities have a decent range of restaurants, and French food can be found just about everywhere.

When eating in a restaurant, prior to the hors-d'œuvre or main course you will be served olives, cold vegetables or salad, and *khubs*, a round flat loaf that, unlike the *pitta* bread found in other Arab countries, is leavened. Most restaurants have a menu in French, which is divided into sections by type of meat (v*iande*): *poulet* (chicken), *bœuf* (beef), or *agneau* (lamb). After the meal, dessert is sometimes available, and it is usual to linger over a cup of coffee or mint tea.

Street Food
Morocco is a culture of munching. Street stalls offer a rich variety of foods for snacking, and no afternoon out would be complete without stopping for at least one of these specialties.

Nuts and Seeds
Almonds, chickpeas, sunflower seeds, peanuts, and other varieties are available and quite

popular. A frequent annoyance is the teenager who leaves the shells of these seeds all over the computer keyboard in the cyber café!

Maqoda

These delicious fried potato balls are spicy and unlike anything found outside the country. They are sometimes available as an appetizer in inexpensive restaurants, and are served with bread.

Brochettes

Grilled meats cooked on a skewer are served throughout Morocco. There are several varieties; *kefta*, lamb, chicken, and spicy *merguez* sausage are all available and served with bread.

Alcohol

Despite being a Muslim country, alcohol is widely available and produced inside Morocco. Expect to pay a significant premium on imported liquors and beer. Wine is produced both in the north and south of the country, with Les Celliers de Meknes leading the pack with several different varieties. Their Guerrouane Rouge is particularly renowned.

Beer is also brewed in-country under the labels Flag Spéciale, Stork, and Casablanca, the latter being the most palatable. Heineken, Amstel, and Corona are also widely available.

Hot Drinks

Coffee is a huge part of Moroccan culture, and excellent espresso is served in nearly all cafés. At home, coffee is either brewed in a *cafetiera* on the stovetop or in an electric coffeemaker, or instant Nescafe is used. Moroccans always sweeten their coffee, but the amount of milk added, if any, varies.

Arabic Name	French Name	Description
Qahua kahela	Café noir Café normal	Black coffee
Qahua mhersa	Café cassé	Coffee with a drop of milk
Nus-nus		Half coffee/half milk
Qahua halib	Café au lait Café crème	Coffee with milk

The national beverage, however, is mint tea. Chinese gunpowder (green) tea is brewed with fresh mint leaves and the finished product is served with copious amounts of sugar. Called *atay* in Moroccan Arabic, it is served by carpet vendors when making a sale, at cafés, at homes, and just about everywhere else you can imagine. As if suddenly aware of the havoc it is wreaking on their teeth, some Moroccans have begun serving it unsweetened, with sugar on the side.

Cold Beverages

Like anywhere else in the world, Coca-Cola (called *Coca*) is on every street corner and in every restaurant. Fanta, Sprite, and Coca Light (a European version of Diet Coke) are also on tap, and the Coca-Cola-owned Poms (apple soda) and Hawai (a tropical fruit-flavored soda) are immensely popular.

Tap water in most of the country, particularly the Middle Atlas and Rif regions, is quite safe and, after a brief settling-in period, you may want to start drinking it. In the meantime, however, several varieties of bottled water are available— Sidi Ali, Sidi Harazem, and Ciel being the most popular. There is also an excellent natural sparkling water bottled under the name of Oulmes (pronounced *wul-mess*).

Orange juice, grape juice, and other juices are also popular, and in many cafés they are served freshly squeezed. Other fruit juices, such as apple, can be purchased easily. Milk is sold under several brands; Jaouda and Salim are the most popular It is traditionally sold refrigerated, but UHT milk, which does not require refrigeration until opened, is also popular. *Leben*, delicious pure buttermilk, is sold fresh and prepackaged; stick to the latter unless you have an iron stomach.

SHOPPING

Morocco is a shoppers' paradise and there is plenty to buy aside from the wonderful rugs and handicrafts. A visit to the *medina* or *souq* often ends up with having to take a taxi home with all your purchases.  Fortunately, Morocco is not a very expensive country, and with some practice, you'll be able to bargain like a native.

Don't expect shopping to be a quick excursion—many shopkeepers will invite you in for tea, and despite the hard sell, most vendors want to please you, as a happy customer is a repeat customer.

Souqs are clusters of markets selling the same types of wares, from household goods to handmade furniture. In cities, *souqs* are typically permanent structures, situated outside the walls of the *medina* as well as inside the labyrinthine streets. In villages, a traveling *souq* often comes once a week—ask to find out on which day.

Leather goods can be found all around the country, but are produced in Fès and Marrakech, which is where you'll find the best deals. The quality of leather is excellent and it is cheap by Western standards, but you should inspect buckles and other metalwork carefully. Gold

jewelry is also comparatively
inexpensive. Silver jewelry is
typically Berber, and
beautiful ornate pieces are
popular with tourists; they
are cheapest in the south,
where most of them are
made. Also of interest is

pottery, produced in Salé and Safi; traditional
Moroccan clothing, which can be purchased "off
the rack" or custom-made; and various traditional
musical instruments, both percussive and string.

Last but not least, no trip to Morocco would be
complete without the purchase of a rug.
Moroccan rugs are appreciated the world over—
and what better way to warm up a spacious, bare
apartment? Buying carpets can involve some hard
bargaining: the trick is to start small. Find a
reputable carpet dealer in your town, and start by
getting to know him over a few glasses of mint
tea. The first time, it is best to start with one small
and inexpensive rug. Shopkeepers appreciate
return customers, and will often give you a deal
the second time around.

It is important to note that tour guides get a
commission for anything you buy in a shop they
introduced you to, so you will certainly be
charged a premium. Also, in the *medinas* of Fès
and other cities, you will often be hounded by

shopkeepers who all seem to know the same seven words in English: "Come have a look at my shop." Don't feel compelled to look until you see something you're truly interested in.

Prices are usually quoted in dirhams, especially to foreigners, but Moroccans often count in centimes, particularly as the numbers get higher. One dirham equals 100 centimes. Therefore, if you're buying a car, the price could be quoted to you as 5 million. Don't fret—5 million centimes is actually 50,000dh, or approximately $5,000. Occasionally, you will also hear a price quoted in riyals. One riyal equals 5 centimes.

Business hours in Morocco are generally from 9:00 a.m. to 12:00 p.m. and from 3:00 to 8:00 p.m. The reason for this three-hour gap is the lunch break, when most Moroccans head home to eat with family. Western-style stores and supermarkets usually stay open during this time, and it's easy to find one or two *hanouts* (see below) that do so as well. On Friday, the main day for prayer, the lunch break is often extended for one hour in either direction.

Food Shopping
When shopping for food, there are several options—you can visit the traveling *souq*, set up somewhat like a farmers market, where food is sold as well as household goods; or you can

choose a store, where prices may be a little higher but supply is dependable. On just about every street lies a *hanout,* a small store selling snacks, beverages, food staples, cigarettes, and other everyday items. Larger *hanouts* are set up like small grocers; others may have items stacked on

shelves behind the counter, requiring you to ask the shopkeeper. *Hanouts* also typically sell fresh bread from the nearest bakery.

Next is the *marché,* a French-style market selling meat, fish, fresh produce, olives, and sometimes even flowers or herbs. The *marché* can be found in the *ville nouvelle* of a city. Finally, the most expensive but probably most convenient way to shop is at the supermarket (*supermarché* in French). Marjane is a huge store reminiscent of Wal-Mart that sells food and a little of everything else. There is one outside most big cities. Another popular *supermarché* is Label Vie, owned by Leader Price. Keep in mind that a heavy tax is often placed on imported foods at these stores.

THE *HAMMAM*

Traditionally, Moroccans did not have showers or baths in their homes. Some still don't, and hot water is often a luxury. Therefore, the *hammam* was and still is the place to get clean and visit with your friends. It is also an excellent respite from drafty apartments during the winter.

Men and women have separate sections in a *hammam*, or in some establishments, separate hours. When going to the *hammam*, you should bring a towel, clean underwear, a low stool to sit on, a bucket, and any toiletries you would normally use during a shower. Moroccans also come prepared with a rough glove or loofah; black soap made from olive resin; *ghassoul*, a thick black clay mixed with herbs and used for degreasing the hair and body; and *henna*, used by women to soften and decorate the hands and feet. These can be bought at some *hammams* for a small fee.

When you enter the *hammam*, the first room you go to is very hot. Here, you will soap up and relax for a while to allow the steam to soften your skin. After a few minutes, you can have a masseur or masseuse scrub you down. Called *gommage* in French, this process can be quite rough and, to the Westerner, can seem immodest as some of the most private areas are scrubbed.

After the hot room, you go straight to a lukewarm room, where women apply *henna* and both genders use *ghassoul*. Though most Moroccans use these products, some also take this time to apply lotion or oil as well. Teeth are brushed, hair is combed and wrapped in a towel, and you are ready to go!

The *hammam* can seem quite daunting at first, but after some getting used to, most foreigners understand why this is a tradition worth keeping. Most Moroccans, whether they have a shower at home or not, attend the *hammam* once a week and consider it the only way to really get clean.

TIPPING

Tipping is a vital part of Moroccan culture. Servers, hotel staff, and the like barely make enough to live on and therefore good service should be rewarded. A 10–15 percent tip is certainly sufficient for restaurant bills; in a café 1–5dh is enough. Tour guides, parking attendants, *hammam* masseurs/masseuses, and anyone else providing you with a minor service should receive a few dirhams.

In smaller cities like Meknes, taxi drivers might charge below the minimum rate for a short journey, in which case a small tip is appropriate. In larger cities, where businesses are used to foreign patrons, it may be best to operate on the percentage system.

OUTDOORS

Morocco is an outdoor lover's paradise. Famous for its mountains and trekking opportunities, there is also plenty to do for the less athletic.

Morocco has over 460 species of bird, making it a favorite destination for bird-watchers. Horse riding is popular, especially in the south, and many cities have an equestrian club, patronized by wealthy Moroccans and foreigners.

Trekking enthusiasts will enjoy Jebel Toubkal, the highest mountain, in the south. Wonderful forest hikes are possible in the Middle Atlas region, particularly near Ifrane and Azrou.

With thousands of miles of coastline, surfing is becoming the rage with young Moroccan men. Agadir, Rabat, and Essaouira are all popular with surfers and have facilities for tourists with rental equipment. Essaouira, dubbed "Windy City Africa," also has windsurfing facilities.

King Mohammed VI is both a golf and Jet Ski enthusiast, and there are several excellent golf courses. Many require membership of particular associations; Web sites detail the requirements.

Last but not least, skiing is picking up speed in Morocco. Oukaïmeden, about 42 miles (68 km) south of Marrakech, is popular with downhill skiers and has the highest ski lift in North Africa. Mischliffen, outside Ifrane, is also well equipped.

chapter seven

TRAVEL, HEALTH, & SAFETY

Getting away from your base occasionally can be quite important. Foreigners staying in Morocco often complain of feeling as though they're living in a goldfish bowl—that everyone is watching them, talking about them, or following them. To the uninitiated, this might seem paranoid, but the truth is that Moroccans are curious by nature and love gossip. It is therefore necessary to take a break every so often, and in a country like Morocco where travel and accommodation are cheap, there's no excuse not to do so!

DRIVING

Morocco has an excellent system of roads, particularly its toll *autoroutes* that run on the Atlantic coast and across to Fès and Meknes. All major cities are connected with good two-lane paved roads, and recently a road has been built leading to Merzouga, on the edge of the Sahara.

Despite the excellent roads, driving can be a nightmare. Moroccan drivers are aggressive, and you could find yourself playing chicken with a truck carrying a load of animals—or worse. On the toll *autoroutes*, however, there are no such problems. Driving at night, particularly between cities, is not recommended, due to the prevalence of drunk drivers.

International and foreign driver's licenses are accepted in Morocco, but if you are an official resident, it is advisable to obtain a Moroccan license, available from the Ministry of Transport.

Car rental is available from major international agencies as well as smaller, Moroccan companies (which are also cheaper). Prices are comparable to those found in Europe, as is gasoline.

Plenty of foreigners get by without a car, as Morocco's public transportation network is both extensive and good.

TRAINS

Though not as fast as its European counterparts, Morocco's train system is consistently good. The state-run company is called ONCF (Office National des Chemins de Fer du Maroc). One line runs from Tangier to Sidi Kacem, where it splits into two—one heading east through Meknes and Fès to Oujda, and another running southwest to Casablanca. The fourth and final line runs from Casablanca to Marrakech. There are new lines linking Safi, Oued Zem, Bouarfa, and El Jadida to the existing network. There has been talk of continuing the line from Marrakech into the Western Saharan Provinces, passing through Agadir and continuing through to Dakhla and Laayoune; for now, a bus service by Supratours connects with train services in Marrakech.

A relatively new high-speed service connects Casablanca and Rabat, and there is now also a train from Casa Voyageurs station in Casablanca that goes directly to the station under Mohammed V airport.

All trains have first- and second-class service, both of which are inexpensive and comfortable. First-class compartments are recommended, as they contain six rather than eight seats, and once a seat is paid for, it is guaranteed. Always pay for your ticket before boarding, as there is a surcharge for purchasing it on board. Train schedules are available in French on the Internet (www.oncf.ma) as well as through a service with Meditel cell phones.

BUSES

Buses travel just about everywhere. CTM, the state-run intercity line, is the most reliable and comfortable. Supratours, a private line affiliated with the ONCF trains, is on par with CTM. Other buses are something of a lottery; some are dependable and safe while others seem quite unstable. They are, however, slightly cheaper. Solo female travelers will feel more comfortable with CTM or Supratours, as the cheaper lines often fill up with men and stop to pick up rural passengers.

Buying tickets in most cities is straightforward, as bus stations are relatively well organized and there are usually officials to assist confused-looking travelers. Ticket prices are generally posted, though they can be negotiated with private companies. As with trains, it is better to buy your ticket before boarding. It is customary to tip anyone who helps you with your luggage.

Larger cities also have local city buses, which are inexpensive and operate on fixed numbered lines. Each city is different, so inquire about the services for where you live. Foreigners and better-off Moroccans prefer to take taxis within cities.

TAXIS, BIG AND SMALL

There are two types of taxi in Morocco—the big intercity taxi, and the small cab used within city centers. During your stay, you will undoubtedly see thousands of each. Both are a reliable and fairly cheap way to get around.

"Big Taxis"

Big taxis, known as *taxi kabir* in Arabic and *grand taxi* in French, are vintage BMWs with a round red medallion on their front grille. They operate mostly on fixed routes between cities and can each carry six passengers (two in front with the driver and four squeezed in the back).

Big taxis congregate at designated taxi stands, usually near bus and train stations, or other city landmarks. Drivers shout the names of their destinations to attract passengers. Don't engage the service of someone who says they'll find a taxi for you unless you're prepared to tip—it should be easy enough to find the proper taxi on your own. The price of a big taxi is negotiable, and you should ask other passengers what they are paying so as to get the proper rate.

If you need to depart immediately and your taxi is not filling up, you can pay the driver for the extra seats and enjoy a ride alone. Solo females often find it desirable to pay for two seats and ride alone with the driver. Additionally, if you would like to take a big taxi to a destination not offered on a fixed route, you need only ask. The taxi driver will have to stop to register with police on his way, and you may be asked for your passport or *carte de séjour*. Prepare to bargain for this type of journey.

"Small Taxis"

Known as *taxi seghir*, or *petit taxi*, these operate within cities only. They are color coded for each city and well-labeled so they are easy to spot. They can be found at designated stations or just hailed on the street. Each can legally carry three passengers, a rule that is strictly enforced.

Small taxis usually have a meter, with an official minimum rate that increases by 50 percent at night. In Casablanca and Marrakech, however, it is common for taxis to operate without meters and it is therefore necessary to haggle for a good rate. Marrakech, in particular, is known for

taxi drivers who shamelessly fleece tourists, and even Moroccans traveling from other cities!

It is possible to hail a taxi that is already carrying another passenger; if he stops for you, the driver will determine the rate, which is usually quite fair (or even in your favor). In general, it is customary to give him a small tip, especially for longer journeys.

AIR TRAVEL

Air travel within Morocco is not cheap, but it is the fastest and most convenient means of travel, particularly to destinations not served by train. The country has fifteen airports, with flights operating daily (or more frequently, depending on destination) from Casablanca. Royal Air Maroc and its new subsidiary, Atlas Blue, as well as a business-oriented service called Regional Airlines, are the only airlines that offer domestic flights.

WHERE TO STAY

With over 3 million visitors a year, Morocco has plenty of hotels to serve all types of travelers. Hotels operate on the five-star system, but this is often applied quite arbitrarily, and a rating of five stars does not guarantee that a hotel will have the requisite amenities of even a three-star hotel.

Big cities have a wide range of accommodation, from five-star hotel chains like Meridien and Hilton to very inexpensive backpacker hotels, some of which are quite pleasant, especially on the tourist circuit. Even small towns will usually have a few options in different price ranges.

When checking in, you will need to show your passport and fill out a form with your personal details. It is technically against the law for unmarried couples to share a hotel room, though this is rarely enforced with foreigners. It is a good idea to carry a copy of your marriage license, however, particularly if one spouse could be mistaken for a Moroccan.

It is quite acceptable to ask to see a room before agreeing to stay, and in smaller hotels it is possible to bargain, particularly if the type of room you want is not available or your room is flawed. It is also always worth asking if there are any discounts, as these are rarely advertised.

Last but not least, it is worth mentioning the *riad*, a uniquely Moroccan experience. In some cities, particularly Fès and Marrakech, Europeans and Moroccans alike have been purchasing and restoring traditional Moroccan homes (*riads*) and turning them into guesthouses. A *riad* is typically decked out in traditional décor and is quite lavish, and prices vary greatly. *Riads* are found exclusively in the *medina*.

PLACES TO VISIT

There are certain must-see destinations that will give the uninitiated a true understanding of Morocco and its fascinating landscape and culture. The following itineraries are merely a taste of what is available.

The Atlantic Coast

If relaxing by the ocean or surfing is your thing, Morocco's Atlantic coast is the place to be. Tangier, longtime home to American author Paul Bowles and current home to hip expatriates and hot nightclubs, is the port where millions of tourists arrive each year from Spain, making it sometimes quite a hassle. Moving southward from Tangier, you'll reach Asilah, an arty town that

holds an international culture festival each year, during which artists from all over the world paint a new mural, covering the one from the year before. Further down the coast you'll reach Rabat and Casablanca, filled with clean family-filled beaches and swanky coastal nightspots.

If Morocco's two largest cities are too fast-paced for your taste, head on a little further until you reach Oualidia, home to arguably the world's best oysters, and El Jadida, a former Portuguese stronghold. After a brief respite, move south until you reach Safi, Morocco's pottery manufacturing capital and factory center. A little further south is Essaouira, where the *Gnaoua* and World Music Festival is held each summer. Essaouira is also extremely popular with windsurfers and hippie types who come to explore the former haunt of rock legend Jimi Hendrix. The last location of note before the Western Sahara, or "Saharan Provinces," is Sidi Ifni, a small town that retains much of its former Spanish flavor.

World Heritage Sites

The *medina* of Fès, also known as Fez al-Bali, is internationally renowned as the world's oldest living and working *medina* and is a UNESCO World Heritage Site. It boasts tanneries operating in the same fashion they have for hundreds of years, as well as labyrinthine streets where even the most seasoned traveler could get lost. If Fès's savvy shopkeepers prove to be too intense, head an hour away to Meknes, also recognized by UNESCO. Here, the imperial city and *medina* have been nicknamed "the Versailles of Morocco." The nearby Roman ruins of Volubilis (Oualili) are a fascinating detour. The *medinas* of both Essaouira and Tetouan are also UNESCO designated sites, as is that of Marrakech. In the south, Aït Benhaddou is a breathtaking *kasbah* (fortress) surrounded by striking mountains. The necropolis of Chellah, outside Rabat, and the Roman ruins of Lixus are also UNESCO World Heritage Sites. An updated list of these sites is available at http://whc.unesco.org.

The South

After any of the major cities, the south of Morocco is a different world. Filled with palm groves, both ruined and restored *kasbahs* (some operating as guesthouses), Berber villages, and deep gorges, it has managed to retain some of the magic lost in the tourist-filled *medinas*. Ouarzazate, the "Hollywood of Morocco," provides flash and excitement, while a drive through the Dadés Valley reveals ancient architecture and oases.

THE ATLAS STUDIOS

In recent years, Ouarzazate's Atlas Studios have become a booming industry for foreign and Moroccan filmmakers alike. *The Sheltering Sky, Gladiator, The Last Temptation of Christ*, and *Kingdom of Heaven* were all shot here. It is possible to visit the studios (www.atlasstudios.com) on locally run tours when shooting is not taking place. You can see the sets used in these films, as well as Egyptian-themed ones and even the Tibetan monastery built for Scorsese's *Kundun*. Other international films shot in Morocco include *Alexander, Spy Game, Rules of Engagement*, and *The Mummy*.

The Souss Valley, home to Morocco's most popular package destination, Agadir, is a magical journey through argan forests, banana groves, and multicolored Berber villages. Cities like Tiznit and Taroudannt offer pure Moroccan-style hospitality without being tourist traps (and are the best places for buying silver Berber jewelry!). After the heat and dust of the desert, the beach towns of Mirleft and Sidi Ifni offer relaxation and surfing.

The Mediterranean Coast

In the north lies the beautiful Mediterranean coastline. Blessed with a temperate climate, this is where many Moroccans take their vacations during the summer months. Restinga Smir and Saidia are up-and-coming resort towns, while Al Hoceima and Oued Laou are slightly off the beaten path. Inland, you can discover Tetouan and its Spanish-influenced *medina*, and the breezy mountain town of Chefchaouen that, while picturesque, is often packed to the brim with European hashish seekers. Foreign residents visit the Spanish enclaves of Ceuta and Melilla to escape Morocco briefly and stock up on the amenities they can't find in-country. Inland and far east is Oujda, a sprawling and rather modern city that was once the gateway to Algeria, but has suffered since the border was closed in 1995.

The Middle Atlas

The Middle Atlas region, which includes the imperial cities of Fès and Meknes, is filled with beautiful cedar forests and small Berber villages. The moment the bus or train leaves the outskirts of these bustling cities, it's a whole other world. The small towns of Ifrane and Azrou boast plenty of green space and wooded areas. Azrou is also the place for inexpensive Berber carpets in a picturesque marketplace. Visit the Roman ruins of Volubilis, then see the town of Moulay Idriss Zerhoun, where Muslim pilgrims travel each year for a large *moussem*. The town is so holy that non-Muslims are not even permitted to spend the night. Sefrou is also a pleasant place to stop, and nearby Bhalil has incredible modern cave-houses and is almost unknown to tourists.

HEALTH

There are some standard dos and don'ts in order to stay healthy in Morocco. In general, it's best not to drink tap water until you've allowed your body a brief period of adjustment. Bottled water is cheap and widely available. Avoid uncooked vegetables when eating out, and be sure to ask for meat to be *bien cuite* (well cooked).

Hepatitis A, spread through contact with contaminated food or water, is present in Morocco and precautions should be taken, particularly in rural areas. Hepatitis B is also quite common; therefore anyone who has intimate contact with Moroccans should be extremely cautious and tested regularly. Vaccination against both hepatitis A and B is highly recommended.

HIV is also present in Morocco, though there is little dependable information on the disease. Though the documented AIDS cases number under one thousand, unsafe sex is rampant and HIV education almost nonexistent. Safe sex should be practiced meticulously. On the positive side, every major city now offers free HIV testing, though this fact is not well-known. Ask a local pharmacist for information.

Various intestinal infections are common in Morocco; food hygiene standards are generally poor, and most foreigners will become infected with some type of stomach bug during their stay. When faced with diarrhea, it is important to keep hydrated—if you suffer a severe attack, you should see a doctor.

Although no vaccinations are required for those coming from Western Europe and the United States, anyone intending to stay in Morocco for an extended period of time should receive vaccinations for diphtheria, tetanus, measles, mumps, rubella, and polio, as well as hepatitis A and B.

Good health care is available in the private sector—larger cities will have at least one foreign-trained doctor, and many doctors speak at least some English. If you have a chronic condition or medicinal allergy of any sort, it is important to know how to talk about it in French or Arabic, or at least carry information about your condition in French on your person at all times.

For dental work, however, it is advisable to have any treatment done before coming to Morocco—there is only one dentist for every eighty thousand residents. For emergencies, good dental care can be found in major cities.

Insurance is advisable, though visits to the doctor are usually inexpensive. Generally, insurance agencies provide a form that you take to the doctor to fill out, and then return to the insurer for reimbursement. Medicines are generally reimbursable as well.

The whole of the country is dotted with pharmacies, and unlike in the United States, pharmacists are able to diagnose minor conditions and sell you medicine on the spot. Most drugs are available without prescription, though in this case they are not reimbursable by most insurers. Prescriptions can be kept and reused numerous times.

SAFETY

Morocco is a safe country and is very accustomed to receiving visitors from other parts of the world. Violent crime is rare even in the biggest cities, and the majority of crime perpetrated against foreigners is petty thievery and pick pocketing. That said, Morocco is a Muslim country, and foreigners who choose to defy the culture and not dress respectably are open to harassment.

Single foreign women often complain of the constant attention. While modest dress and dark glasses go a long way in avoiding this, Moroccan men often take advantage of your presence and say "hello." After all, what do they have to lose? It is of course polite to say "hello" back and keep walking. If someone takes it a step further and follows you, respect is the operative word—telling a man that he is disrespecting you will usually make him leave, or even apologize. If nothing else works, say "*seer f-halek*," a term that is considered vulgar by Moroccans but means "go away." Otherwise alert a police officer or even a shopkeeper.

chapter eight

BUSINESS BRIEFING

Morocco has vast natural resources, an excellent geographic position, and an investment climate that favors foreign investors. The economy is liberal and in a state of flux. The main sectors are tourism, phosphates mining, agriculture, and commercial fishing. Tourism is one of the fastest growing sectors, with a target of 10 million tourists a year by 2010.

The growing of cannabis, though technically illegal, has traditionally been one of the main currency earners in the Rif mountains. Under pressure from the E.U. and the U.S.A., the Moroccan government has launched an initiative to eliminate production by 2015. Legitimate agricultural exports are fruits and vegetables bound for Europe, including dates and nuts.

THE BUSINESS CULTURE

Moroccan culture is heavy on hospitality; in fact, this is widely regarded as a social obligation. Expect mint tea to be served early and often.

Business moves at a slower pace than in the West, with an emphasis on relationships, rather than tasks. In short, it's not *what* you know, it's *who* you know that makes things work. Far from being a waste of time, developing relationships and friendships is crucial to doing business here. Foreigners are often surprised by how quickly they can make contacts in one single meeting.

Moroccans love to be helpful and once a relationship is established, people will often put themselves out to help you achieve your objective. It is important to be patient in regards to Moroccan timekeeping; being punctual indicates seriousness, but time is flexible in Morocco and "on time" is a relative concept. If you ask a contact to help you with something, they will often volunteer to do it immediately; it is wise to take them up on it because the next opportunity may be a long time in coming.

Moroccan bureaucracy is formidable and labyrinthine. A good network can help to cut through red tape and put you in contact with others who can clear obstacles for you. The bureaucracy is based on French administrative practices and customs—observing protocol is crucial, and courtesy and formality are the rule.

Family is important and Moroccans often carry pictures of themselves and their family. Pointed questions about age and family status are normal and socially acceptable, even in a business setting. Business customs vary from region to region, however, and you can expect business in the urban centers to be much more Westernized.

THE LANGUAGE OF BUSINESS

Though the first language of most Moroccans is *derija* and proficiency will gain you respect, French tends to be the language of business. Modern Standard Arabic is also commonly used. If you are investing in Morocco and don't speak either language, you will certainly run into difficulties—it may be best to engage the services of a Moroccan assistant early on, or hire an interpreter. English will only be helpful in the tourism sector.

HOURS AND SCHEDULES

Although officially there has been a movement toward "continuous hours," this has not really taken hold. Most shops (aside from Western-style supermarkets) are open from 9:00 or 10:00 a.m. until noon or 1:00 p.m.; they close until about 3:00 p.m., and then stay open until about 9:00 in the evening. Even at a place that supposedly observes continuous hours, it is often difficult to accomplish much at the lunch hour. Lunch is the major meal of the day and socially important. Expect to be invited for Friday *couscous* by even casual acquaintances. Friday is the holy day and most stores and offices are closed after noon.

Major holidays include *Ramadan*, when business tends to grind to a virtual halt. Nightlife is vibrant during this holiday, but most bars and all liquor stores are closed for the month. People fast all day and could not be described as being "on top of their game." Publicly eating and drinking during the day is impolite; drinking alcohol is highly frowned upon. August is the traditional holiday month, and nearly everyone heads for the beach for at least part of it. *Eid al-Kabir* and *Eid al-Seghir* are also major religious holidays when most business activities cease.

OFFICE ETIQUETTE AND PROTOCOL
Business Dress
Moroccans tend to judge others on appearances, so it is in your best interest to dress well and pay close attention to grooming details, such as polished shoes. Moroccans notice details. Business dress is generally conservative and formal. Dark, classic suits with conservative ties are the norm for men. Suits, dresses, or pantsuits that are

elegant but conservative are best for women. It is important for women to be appropriately covered, with skirts below the knee (worn with hose or tights) and long sleeves. Clothes should not be tightly fitted and jackets that cover the hips are advised; a sharp pantsuit with a long jacket is ideal. Accessories should be minimal and not ostentatious. Designer labels are highly regarded and even casual dress should be snappy.

Be Flexible

Morocco is a Muslim country, albeit one of the more liberal, and the law and culture reflect this. Moroccan culture embraces a wide variety of customs and observances, by region and by individual. Be prepared to adapt. Although you will encounter Moroccans who are not strict in their religious observances, be prepared to discreetly accommodate those who are. It is obligatory for a Muslim to pray five times a day and it is courteous and respectful to allow space and time for this practice. If someone steps away from a meeting to pray, simply carry on your business quietly and resume without comment when your companion returns.

Self-Control and Saving Face

Relationships and friendships are critical and group work is favored over individual effort.

Harmony and politeness are highly valued; regardless of circumstances, staying cool and speaking moderately and politely is appreciated. Self-control is both respected and rewarded. To preserve the peace, minor (and sometimes major) "untruths" are both accepted and expected. Personal honor is important, as is seniority, and it is important to understand the hierarchy of your environment. *Hshuma* is to be avoided at all costs in business situations. Keeping up appearances is important and *hshuma* occurs when other people are aware of a failure or inappropriate action.

Public actions are designed to enhance personal standing and avoid social discomfort or embarrassment. It is considered shameful to admit that one doesn't know or is unable to do something. "*Mashi mushkil*" (no problem) is a phrase you will hear often: it should be taken with a grain of salt. It is not uncommon for these to be the last words you hear from someone who may then avoid you because he cannot fulfill his commitment. It is wise to ensure that agreements are verified and witnessed by others. Once a friendship is established, you should be prepared to both give and receive assistance, as this is an expected part of the relationship. Strict separation of personal and professional lives is virtually nonexistent. Make time for developing relationships if you want to get anything done.

Politeness

Modesty is also highly valued. Be polite and respectful to everyone, because it is possible to meet a very powerful and valuable contact who would not dream of telling you about their position. This is left to their entourage. It is considered bad form to brag about or overstate one's influence or accomplishments. If you encounter someone who is doing this, proceed with caution. It seems that the more powerful and influential someone is, the less they advertise their position. Inquiring discreetly of others can yield a lode of valuable information; Moroccans love to gossip and are proud of their networks.

Business Cards

Business cards are commonly used, and those wishing to do business in Morocco are well advised to include a French translation of the content. Including an Arabic translation is a sign of respect. Any correct use of the Arabic language is usually met with delight and significant business advantages can follow. Present the card with the translation facing the recipient.

Business Gifts

To cultivate business relationships, gifts are readily exchanged for any reason or for no reason at all. Exchange is an important part of this practice and should be moderately discreet. There is a certain protocol to gift giving. It is important not to be excessively generous as "a gift demands a gift," and it is equally *hshuma* for a person to be unable to repay a kindness. It is not uncommon for gifts to be very thoughtful, and if you openly admire something someone is wearing, for example, you may find it offered to you on the spot or receive a similar gift later.

Small, exquisite gifts are much appreciated, such as choice dates from the south to people in northern regions; framed photos of important meetings or outings; and anything imported, especially from your hometown. In short, anything that makes a thoughtful personal link is a good business gift. Anything alcoholic could be offensive. Sweet pastries, dates, or figs are excellent gifts to bring when invited for a meal, as are small items for children. Gifts are often not opened at the time they are presented, so don't be offended if your host immediately puts your gift aside without mention.

LEADERSHIP AND DECISION MAKING
Moroccan business is top-down; however, directors and managers generally rely on a team of advisors and usually have a right-hand person

who may sit in on meetings. Protocol is important here and the hierarchical code demands great regard for the person in charge. Moroccans will not generally contradict their superiors and may tell them what they think they want to hear. Saving face is important and directly accepting blame is uncommon. Blame must be placed somewhere, however, and lower-level employees often take the hit. Employees will often hesitate to take a position or give an opinion; taking a stand can invite blame or criticism, so many avoid it outright. It is generally accepted that the person in charge will give specific instructions and these instructions and limits of authority will be followed carefully. Bounds are rarely overstepped, and honest input can be hard to come by.

Unemployment is high and a young, educated workforce is readily available. The traditional business environment does not encourage individuality, and the "groupthink" mentality is common; however, employees are often eager to please and can be encouraged to give opinions and make decisions in specific defined contexts.

MEETINGS AND NEGOTIATIONS

Although it is necessary to make appointments several days in advance, and to call to verify the day before, it is also wise to schedule yourself loosely. Business does not generally function according to a Western model of efficiency. Allow time for lateness, missed appointments, and delays in completing or accomplishing things. A rule of thumb is always to be prompt yourself, but to be somewhat flexible about punctuality in others. Also allow time for obligatory courtesies, such as discussion about family and other friendly chat. A simple meeting over coffee can result in opportunities for other introductions or contacts that are best seized in the moment. Despite the difference in the pace of doing business, there is a strong undercurrent of "Do It Now!"—failure to act can mean an opportunity lost.

Meetings

Schedule meetings as far in advance as possible and allow plenty of time. Friday afternoon is generally not the best time to meet, nor any day during *Ramadan*. Expect interruptions, as an open-door policy is generally observed, and others may join you to discuss unrelated matters. Be patient, and don't try to redirect the discussion to the original topic until the newcomer leaves. Business is generally done in French, so establish in advance whether you will need an interpreter.

During introductions, men will often introduce themselves by their first name, while everyone else calls them by their last. Names are also given quickly, last name first. A basic familiarity with Arabic names can make this go more smoothly and help you to remember names. Use formal address, unless and until the other person invites you to do otherwise. *Sidi* is the term of respect, equivalent to "Mister."

Presentation and Listening Styles
Presentations tend to be formal and one is expected to listen politely to the information being delivered. Texts are often read, and questions should be held until the end of the presentation. Questions should be indirect and polite and sensitive issues may be best dealt with more privately. Audiovisual aids and handouts impress and suggest seriousness and preparation, but be careful to avoid ostentation or anything that may make others believe you are trying to outdo them or make them feel inferior.

Lengthy deliberation over decisions is the norm, and at times it may seem that no one wants to accept responsibility for finding the solution. Innovation and bold speech are in general not favorably regarded. Government negotiations entail more protocol and political maneuvering (and time) to be sure that all the relevant officials have been consulted, and positions respected. Take time and be patient in order to avoid insults.

Several meetings may be required to accomplish even simple things. Remember, Moroccans tend to be conservative and interested in long-term relationships.

Read Between the Lines

Direct confrontation and criticism are frowned upon and preservation of honor is crucial. Guard the honor of your associates and try not to do anything that might cause them to lose face. Recognize also that in negotiations, others may insincerely agree with you to prevent *you* from losing face. When dealing with new relationships or social superiors, see how others' contributions are received in order to gauge the extent to which you should participate.

Negotiating Styles

When dealing with finance, be prepared to haggle and leave a bargaining margin in initial offers. You should expect your Moroccan counterparts to build a haggling margin into any quotes you receive. Offers only become final after much discussion and negotiation. Although Moroccans can be shrewd and skillful negotiators, and may pressure you, high-pressure tactics on your part tend to backfire. The person with the highest rank makes the final decision, but only after thorough discussion with other members of the group.

CONTRACTS

As in any business environment, contracts are important. However, a contract is only as good as the relationship between the parties involved. If there is a lack of trust, the contract will not hold. The bureaucracy of the justice system is complicated at best; therefore you should carefully consult with a Moroccan legal advocate before entering into any agreement. A contract should be regarded as a manifestation of the trust established between you and your associate.

WOMEN IN MANAGEMENT

Women are now moving into management positions, but the transition is slow. Western women doing business in Morocco will be well served by conservative dress and a serious, formal approach. Men should greet Moroccan women politely and only shake hands if the woman offers hers. Formal address (*Mademoiselle* or *Madame* with the family name) should be used. Excessive eye contact is considered impolite and in bad taste. Do not expect female colleagues to attend evening meetings except in liberal urban areas. Many women prefer to return home early at night in order to avoid the *hshuma* that could occur if they were seen returning late.

CANDOR AND COOPERATION

As we have seen, social harmony and respect are often fueled by white lies. These may be employed to protect the honor of a superior, of the speaker, or of you yourself, whether you want it or not. It may be necessary to relax your standards of truthfulness. Direct speech is considered rather impolite and criticisms and points of disagreement are expressed obliquely (if at all). Commitments can be made to save face and keep you happy, regardless of whether they can be honored. Timetables are often unrealistic; always allow a generous margin for the vagaries of Moroccan business practice.

It is rare to hear Moroccans say, "I don't know." This would entail a loss of face, so rather than admitting it outright, they may give you their best guess. A direct "No" is also uncommon—instead, a Moroccan may avoid or change the subject in order not to offend. Be aware that when the talk turns to specifics, you may be facing a tough adversary. The transition can be quite startling.

TEAMWORK AND MANAGEMENT

Due to widely varying practices and the continuing evolution of Morocco's business culture, it is best to take your time and observe your Moroccan counterparts closely in order to get an idea of the extent of their acceptance of Western business practices. Try to avoid criticizing the local norms. Many employees are eager and willing to rise to a challenge and fulfill their potential. Try to spot natural leaders and progressive thinkers on your team. Cultivating their skills and talents can help lead the way to a shift in group dynamics and greater efficiency. Encouraging risk tolerance is also helpful in building a dynamic team. There is a tendency to resist change, but Moroccans can be extremely adaptable when change is introduced skillfully. Cultural sensitivity and team-building skills are important tools.

If a problem arises, don't expect anyone to take responsibility, especially in public. Blame shifting is widely practiced. More time may be spent in placing blame than in resolving the problem.

FOREIGN INVESTMENT

Morocco is actively trying to attract foreign investors and has undertaken initiatives to modernize, privatize, and generally adhere to internationally accepted business and accounting practices. Reforms have been carried out in the areas of labor law, commercial law, and corporate law. Government incentives to foreign investors

include an agency to provide information on its liberal tax exemptions and investment subsidies.

The regulatory environment is liberal, although the bureaucracy can be daunting and the justice system inconsistent. Direct investments can be freely transferred without special authorization, and there are no limits placed on the amount of investment revenue transferred out of the country. Foreign investors have the same rights as local investors and are not required to obtain any special authorization to sell their investments. Transfer of funds is straightforward and can be made in foreign currencies or convertible dirhams. All foreigners have the right to open a bank account in Morocco.

There are complex regulations governing the establishment of an enterprise—you should research these carefully and develop a relationship with a good Moroccan corporate legal advocate. Your network will be invaluable in this effort. Customarily, bribes have been the grease for the squeaky wheel, but this practice is no longer widespread and is not encouraged.

Tax laws favor investment and were reformed in 1984 in the interest of transparency, clarity, and simplicity. Taxes include corporate tax, value added tax, income tax, and return on shares tax. There are numerous sites available on the Internet with up-to-date information on tax rates, regulations, trade agreements, and incentives.

chapter nine

COMMUNICATING

LANGUAGE

As we have seen, the lingua franca of Morocco is a dialect of Arabic called Maghrebi Arabic or simply *derija*. In theory, all Moroccans learn French from the second grade; however, the reality is that in the countryside many native Berber speakers are already struggling to learn Arabic as a second language and French becomes tertiary. In the major cities, you will be surprised to find that many shopkeepers, particularly those selling carpets, have taught themselves English. English is growing as a third (or fourth) language—it is now taught in most high schools and the American Cultural Assocation–sponsored American Language Centers are located in eight cities and expanding. The British Council provides classes in Casablanca as well. Additionally, Spanish is spoken in the Rif and Mediterranean regions, and in cities like Chefchaouen it can be more common than even French.

GREETINGS

No Moroccan conversation would be complete without an extended greeting, the content of which is approximately as follows:

Salaam aleikum: May peace be upon you.
Waleikum salaam: And upon you as well.

Labas? Labas alik?: *Labas* literally means "no harm" and as a question implies, "How are things?" *Labas alik* asks more specifically about your personal well-being.
Labas, alhamdulillah: No harm, thanks be to God.

Bekhair?: Literally meaning "fine," this question asks, "Are you well?"
Bekhair: Fine [the response].

Kolshi muzien?: *Kolshi* means "everything." Therefore, as a question, this means, "Is everything good?"
Muzien: Good [the response].

The first speaker will then continue to ask about the second speaker's family and health, and then the roles reverse. This greeting is often done at warp speed, sometimes without even slowing one's pace if on the street. Foreigners living in Morocco will quickly be inducted into this tradition even if they do not speak Arabic. It is useful to learn the proper responses; you may even find people patiently "feeding" them to you.

Between men, handshakes are a standard greeting, and once a friendship is established, a handshake and a kiss on both cheeks, starting with the left, are expected. After shaking hands, it is customary to place your hand over your heart. Close friends will exchange four kisses. Between women, the handshake and kiss are also standard.

If you are a man greeting a woman, allow her to take the lead: if she extends her hand, shake it. If she doesn't, don't take it personally; she may simply be very devout and physical contact is *haram* for her. The same goes if you are a woman greeting a bearded man: if your hand is not taken, it is probably due to religious scruple. Men and women do not generally greet one another with kisses unless they are very close. In a business setting, this is clearly inappropriate.

When joining a group of people it is customary to shake hands, starting with the person on your right, and introductions are usually made at this time. At a large social gathering, it is acceptable to simply say, "*Salaam aleikum*" and make eye contact with the others. Try to say good-bye to each person individually when you are leaving.

BODY LANGUAGE

Moroccans are generally quite affectionate and tactile. Remember, however, that in public this is only true between members of the same sex. Thus members of the same sex will normally kiss one another on each cheek when greeting, with women often drawing this out to three or four kisses.

Of course, this is often different for the younger generation, who will greet close friends of the opposite sex with a kiss on the cheek.

A handshake between men frequently lasts throughout the entire conversation. Both men and women quite often hold hands or link arms while walking with same-sex friends. This does not in any way indicate a homosexual relationship; it is considered completely natural.

As in other Arab societies, it is important to be careful with one's left hand—the left hand is used for personal hygiene. When eating, Moroccans will only use their right hand to take food from a common dish. When eating from your own plate, however, it is almost always acceptable to eat with either or both hands. The only exception might be in very rural areas— wait and see what others are doing. Incidentally, Moroccans who are born left-handed tend to write with their left hand but learn to do everything else with their right.

GESTURES AND TABOOS
Dos

- A nod of the head means "yes" but a shake of the head can mean "no" or "I'm not sure."
- A shrug of the shoulders expresses the feeling "What can I do about it?"
- If someone is thirsty or wants water, they will put an outstretched thumb to their lips.
- After shaking hands, Moroccans will place their right hand over their heart for a moment.
- Two index fingers placed side by side indicate *kif-kif*, or "same," and can also imply friendship or a relationship.
- One finger pulling down the lower eyelid indicates *hshuma* (shame).
- To indicate "Come here," the whole hand is used rather than one finger.
- Shaking one's hand next to the head or ear indicates "crazy," usually in reference to another person.

Don'ts

- Raising or lowering the middle finger at someone is an obscene gesture.
- Creating a circle with the thumb and index finger, which indicates "OK" in other countries, actually means "zero" or "bad" in Morocco.

TOPICS OF CONVERSATION

There are several topics of conversation that are best avoided, including criticism of the King or royal family, the Israel-Palestine conflict, the disputed Western Sahara, and sexual etiquette.

Topics that are not taboo and may result in an interesting and lengthy discussion are emigration and the "brain drain," the Moroccan education system, and certain subjects related to Islam (such as the banning of the *hijab* in French schools)—assuming you agree with the Moroccan point of view, that is! General discussion of the royal family is no longer taboo, but be careful not to discuss individual members too personally.

Finally, topics that are generally safe include music, television, and entertainment; travel within or outside Morocco; food; your experiences in Morocco or abroad; and your appreciation of Islam.

SERVICES
Telephone
Landline phones are not common in Morocco as they are expensive and difficult to install, and cell phones are quite cheap and widely available, as are public pay phones. There are two cell-phone companies, Meditel and Maroc Telecom (also called IAM); opinion is divided as to which is the

best. Calls between the two companies are more expensive than within the same network, however, and it is worth noting that Maroc Telecom is the more popular of the two. It is possible to purchase a monthly cell-phone subscription; however, most people opt to use prepaid cards, which come in denominations ranging from 10dh to 2,500dh or more and can be purchased from any *tabac* or *hanout*. To activate the card, you must either call a number and enter a code or send an SMS message containing the code—both options are detailed on the back of the card. Cell phones in Morocco are all GSM and work just about everywhere in the country. European-bought cell phones usually work; however, American ones (even those that are multiband and unlocked) are hit and miss.

There are four area codes related to region, which cover the following zones: Casablanca-Settat, Rabat-Tangier, Marrakech-Laayoune, and Fès-Oujda. There are also several telephone codes dedicated solely to cell phones, which are quickly outnumbering landlines in Morocco.

Pay phones are extremely modern and require a prepaid card, which is inserted into the front of the phone. These cards, called Kalimat, are available in various denominations for either internal or international calls. It is generally cheaper to use a Kalimat to make an international call than it is to make one using a cell phone.

The last option, which you will certainly use at some point, is the *téléboutique*. These "phone offices" offer coin-operated phones and there is generally an attendant to give change or help you dial the number. It is less expensive to make a call from a *téléboutique* than it is to use your cell phone, and many Moroccans do this, using their cell phones for incoming calls only (which are, incidentally, free).

It is worth noting that it is more expensive to call a Moroccan cell phone from abroad than it is to call a landline phone.

IMPORTANT TELEPHONE NUMBERS
The operator will reply in Arabic, or sometimes in French.
Ambulance 15
Police 19
Gendarmerie **(rural police)** 177
Fire 16
Directory Assistance 160
International Directory Assistance 126

Internet
Internet cafés are available in all cities and in some small towns. They are inexpensive for the

casual user and at most of them it is possible to gain a cheaper rate by signing up for a prepaid card with the attendant. For those who want the Internet at home, ADSL is now available through Menara and Maroc Telecom, and seems to be rapidly replacing the once-popular Wanadoo dial-up service. It is also fairly inexpensive.

Moroccans are extremely computer-savvy, which can be both an advantage and a disadvantage. When using a cyber café, it is always a good idea to clear the cache and history, and you should be very cautious when using credit cards to place online orders, as hackers abound.

Mail
Sending mail from Morocco is relatively straightforward and reliable, but when receiving mail, this is not always the case. Packages in particular are  often held up at customs in Rabat or Casablanca, and the recipient occasionally has to travel to obtain the package in person.

When sending mail from Morocco, you will visit *al-bosta*, or "La Poste" in French. This is the place for purchasing stamps, sending letters, buying tax stamps when required for documents, and sending telegrams.

A typical address within a Moroccan city would be written like this:

Lamiae El Aichaoui
Bis Rue Zekkat, Appartement 12
3ème étage, Ville Nouvelle
Meknès, Maroc 50000

Country and village addresses are less formatted, and can include fun phrases like "behind the mosque" or "next to the butcher."

THE MEDIA
Television
Wandering through the *medina*, it would seem that even the poorest neighborhoods are covered in satellite dishes. Though a television, satellite dish, and decoder can be quite expensive, it's a one-time fee and brings a great return! Television is also the most popular source of news, and satellite stations are in no way censored (evident in the number of adult channels available).

There are two state channels and hundreds of imported ones offering a variety of programming in a host of languages. Satellite brings at least seven music channels from the Middle East, Europe, and

the U.S.A. (including both American and European MTV) and at least ten other channels in English, including CNN, BBC World, and the Disney Channel.

Radio

There is a good selection of radio stations providing both music and news. Moroccan stations, both AM and FM, feature Moroccan music, popular Arabic music mostly from Egypt, and Western popular music. There is news programming in French, Arabic, and even Berber, and with a short- or long-wave radio, you can pick up international stations such as the BBC World Service.

Print

Newspapers in Arabic and French are widely available and cheap. If you are sitting in a café, you can purchase a few for a miniscule fee that will be returned to you upon leaving. Unfortunately, there are few papers or magazines available in English. European *Time* and *Newsweek*, *The Economist* and the *International Herald Tribune* (complete with inserted English edition of the Spanish paper *El País*) are usually easy to locate, and the *Daily Mirror* is occasionally available. There is also a range of French glossies, on every topic from interior design to yoga.

There is one monthly English newspaper called the *Messenger of Morocco* but it is nearly impossible to find outside Fès, where it is published. There is also an excellent online newspaper at www.moroccotimes.com, which covers a wide range of topics.

CONCLUSION

Few societies have changed as much as Morocco in such a short period of time. In the past hundred years, Moroccans have witnessed the rise and fall of a colonial empire, have seen their country granted independence, and have experienced landmark changes in the way the country is governed.

With so many changes, there are bound to be setbacks. For example, the 20 percent unemployment rate has resulted in a "brain drain" as educated Moroccans make their way abroad, and a fundamentalist interpretation of Islam is gaining ground among the urban poor. Still, as technology becomes widespread and the world shrinks further, Morocco is slowly coming into its own.

The magic of Morocco has enchanted countless foreigners. The call of the *muezzin* seems to draw people from every corner of the globe to experience Moroccan culture firsthand. Edith Wharton, in her famous book *In Morocco*, wrote, "In Morocco the dream-feeling envelops one at every step." Though today's Morocco is quite different from the one Wharton experienced at the turn of the nineteenth century, most foreigners will nod their heads in recognition of that "dream-feeling."

Morocco isn't always the easiest place to get to know. For the uninitiated foreigner, the bureaucracy can be maddening, the language impossible, and getting to know Moroccans a constant source of frustration. But if you learn to accept things as they are and go with the flow, you'll discover the legendary hospitality, curiosity, and kindness that Moroccans are known for. If you let Morocco into your heart, you'll find that it embraces you right back.

Appendix: A Phonetic Guide to the Arabic Alphabet

ا	alif	*the long vowel aa*	ض	daad	*d (emphatic d)*
ب	baa	*b*	ط	ta	*t (emphatic t)*
ت	taa	*t*	ظ	dhaal	*dh (emphatic dh)*
ث	thaa	*th (soft English th)*	ع	ayn	*'ayn (glottal as in "uh-oh")*
ج	jeem	*dj (soft, as in genre)*	غ	ghayn	*r, gh (strong uvular r like German)*
ح	ha	*ha (heavily aspirated h sound)*	ف	feh	*f*
خ	kha	*kh (like Spanish jota)*	ق	qaaf	*q*
د	daal	*d*	ك	kaaf	*k*
ذ	dhal	*dh (hard English th)*	ل	laam	*l*
ر	ra	*r (rolled r)*	م	meem	*m*
ز	zain	*z*	ن	noon	*n*
س	seen	*s*	ه	ha	*h (breathy h)*
ش	sheen	*sh*	و	waaw	*w, oo*
ص	saad	*s (emphatic s)*	ي	yaaw	*y, ee*

Resources

Al Akhawayn University
BP 104, Ave Hassan II
Ifrane 53000
Tel: 055 86 20 00
Web site: www.aui.ma
Morocco's only English-language university offers resources for learning Arabic, conferences on micro-business, and other social issues, in addition to providing a world-class education.

Alif Fes
Web site: www.alif-fes.com
Offers long-term and intensive Arabic courses.

American Cultural Association
4 Rue Tanger
Rabat
Tel: 037 76 12 69
Web site: www.aca.org.ma
Cultural association that oversees the American Language Centers.

Maghreb Arts
Web site: www.maghrebarts.ma
Provides information (in French) on Moroccan art, theater, music, and festivals in Morocco.

Morocco FAQ and Information
Web site: www.moroccosavvy.com
Maintained by Jan van der Erf, this site offers the most comprehensive Morocco travel information in English on the Web.

ONMT (Office National Marocain du Tourisme/National Tourist Office)
Rue Oued El Makhazine
Rabat
Tel: 037 67 37 56
Web site: www.visitmorocco.com
Morocco's official National Tourist Office, with bureaux in all major cities.

ONCF (Office National des Chemins de Fer/National Rail Service)
Web site: www.oncf.ma
Lists train schedules and fares in both French and Arabic.

Further Reading

Abouzeid, Leila. *Year of the Elephant: A Moroccan Woman's Journey Toward Independence*. Austin, Tex.: Center for Middle Eastern Studies, University of Austin, 1989.

Bacon, Dan, and Andjar Bichr. *Lonely Planet Moroccan Arabic Phrasebook*. Victoria: Lonely Planet Publications, 1999.

Bennani-Smirès, Latifa. *Moroccan Cooking*. Casablanca: Société d'Edition et de Diffusion Al Madariss, 2005.

Bentahila, Abdelali. *Language Attitudes Among Arabic-French Bilinguals in Morocco*. New York: Henry Holt & Co., 1983.

Bowles, Paul. *Their Heads Are Green and Their Hands Are Blue*. New York: Ecco Press, 1994.

Fouré, Catherine, et al. (eds.). *Knopf Guide Morocco*. Toronto/New York: Alfred A. Knopf (Random House), 2003.

Hardy, Paula, et al. *Lonely Planet: Morocco*. London/Oakland/Victoria: Lonely Planet Publications, 2005.

Harrell, Richard S., et al. *A Basic Course in Moroccan Arabic*. Washington, D.C.: Georgetown University Press, 2003.

Hibbard, Allen. *Paul Bowles. Magic and Morocco*. San Francisco: Cadmus Editions, 2004.

Kerper, Barrie. *Morocco: The Collected Traveler*. New York: Fodor's, 2001.

Mayne, Peter. *A Year in Marrakesh*. New York: Hippocrene Books, 1982.

Mernissi, Fatima. *Beyond the Veil*. Bloomington, Ind.: Indiana University Press, 1985.

———. *Dreams of Trespass: Tales of a Harem Girlhood*. Cambridge, Mass.: Perseus Books, 1994.

Pennell, C. R. *Morocco Since 1830: A History*. New York: New York University Press, 2001.

Waterbury, John. *The Commander of the Faithful*. New York: Columbia University Press, 1970.

Complete Arabic: The Basics. New York: Living Language, 2005.

culture smart! morocco

Index

Acknowledgments

I would like to thank Mustapha for his tireless support, Jan for always having the answers, and Laurel, my business guru, without whom this book would not have been possible.